THE COMPLETE GUIDE TO **Night**
& Lowlight
Digital Photography

D1514476

THE
COMPLETE
GUIDE TO Night
& Lowlight
Digital Photography

MICHAEL FREEMAN

ILEX

First published in the United Kingdom in 2008 by:

I L E X

The Old Candlemakers

West Street

Lewes

East Sussex BN7 2NZ

www.ilex-press.com

Publisher: Alastair Campbell

Creative Director: Peter Bridgewater

Rights Director: Roly Allen

Managing Editor: Chris Gatcum

Senior Editor: Adam Juniper

Art Director: Julie Weir

Designer: Chris and Jane Lanaway

Design Assistant: Emily Harbison

British Library Cataloguing-in-Publication Data

A catalogue record for this book is available from the British Library.

ISBN 1-905814-23-2

ISBN 978-1-905814-23-7

Printed and bound in China

For more information on this title please visit:

www.web-linked.com/cglouk

CONTENTS

SECTION 3
LOCKED DOWN 158

INTRODUCTION

In previous books, by and large I've divided the subject between shooting and post-production, a logical sequence that starts with the actual photography and moves through to the various ways of managing and optimizing images on the computer. The skills are different, as is the place and time, and so this makes sense. Here, however, I deliberately mix post-production and computer work in with the shooting. I've taken a conscious decision to do this because it seems to me that time is moving on and digital photography is no longer a new, high-tech version of old photography. For most photographers it is now photography, pure and simple. Moreover, I'm thinking about who the audience for this book is. Lowlight photography is specialized, and certainly more demanding technically than most other forms. I think it less likely that you will dive straight into this as your first serious experience in photography than the more predictable route—exploring a new area having already mastered the basic techniques. Here I have stepped right over these basic techniques, and have skipped the primer stage of setting up the computer, familiarizing yourself with image editors like Photoshop, and so on. For anyone who was expecting this, I apologize, but would direct them towards other volumes like *The Complete Guide to Digital Photography*.

Also, dealing with software and post-production in the same breath as shooting techniques more accurately reflects the way that professionals shoot. A theme I've probably worn threadbare in other books is that successful digital photography above all demands anticipation—knowing in advance what you can do later in post-production. Nevertheless, I'll repeat it here, because lowlight photography in particular has to deal with the limits of acceptable imagery, There is a good deal of problem-solving involved in this kind of photography, and a large part of the work has to happen on the computer. So, it's essential to know at the time of shooting just how much, for example, you can expect to open up dark shadows or recover highlights from a streetlamp.

SECTION 1
LOW LIGHT

The ends of the day, life indoors and the entire range of nighttime activities offer a rich and large source of subjects for photography, now more accessible than ever before. And it is digital photography, with its many continuing advances that has made it more accessible. What we are talking about here is extending the shooting range into situations that, because of insufficient light, could not be handled as freely as film photographers would have liked.

Photography has always had technical limits, but then photographers have always learned to accommodate and to work within them. In fact, they are not always thought of at the time as limits, and it is only when these are about to be broken, or have just been broken, by technological improvements that we can see just how restricting they have been. The quantity of light and the sensitivity of the recording medium has always been one of the most basic limitations. In the early days of photography, it restricted shooting to bright daylight, and even then the exposure times were not short. As film emulsions improved in sensitivity, and as lenses became faster and cameras smaller, it became possible, but only just, to shoot in artificial light.

The first photojournalist was, arguably, Eric Salomon, who made use of the 1924-designed Ermanox 858. This camera, designed by Ludwig Bertele, a maximum aperture of $f1.8$ and shutter speeds up to 1/1200 second, making it possible to capture Salomon's celebrated "candid" pictures of society life in Berlin. Developments were rapid, and Lecia soon announced a camera with similar capabilities that accepted the more convenient 35mm film rather than rigid plates.

Digital photography and its recent changes have ushered in a new era in lowlight photography by extending the range of time and situations that can reasonably be captured, making it possible to use a camera under conditions that would have been unthinkable without resorting to invasive techniques such as flash and artificial setups. Sensor sensitivity has improved hugely in recent years and this, combined with in-camera and post-production processing, has reduced the collateral damage to images from noise—a major preoccupation in this kind of shooting and in this book. In this first chapter, we'll look at how the digital process—from sensor to in-camera processing, to post-processing—handles light when it comes in quantities significantly less than during a normal day.

LIGHT ON THE SENSOR

As we'll see throughout this book, lowlight photography pushes limits. It pushes the limits of technique, demanding constant attention to steadying the camera, subject movement, and changing camera settings to suit the conditions. It also pushes the technical limits, beginning with the sensor and lens. The special conditions found in many lowlight situations tend to highlight sensor deficiencies. Notable among these are blooming and noise. In effect, these operate at opposite ends of the brightness range; blooming is flare surrounding over-exposed highlights, while digital noise is at its most apparent in the shadows, in longer exposures, or at higher sensitivities.

The new digital capabilities for capturing images in low light depend ultimately on sensor performance and the several ways in which camera manufacturers both enhance and manage this.

Blooming is the leakage from a photosite on the sensor that has reached full well capacity (complete white) into adjacent photosites. High quality sensors show less of this than cheaper ones, but some flaring is inevitable in the typical lowlight situation where there are bright lights against dark backgrounds. The city night view here is typical. Nevertheless, we are so accustomed to seeing flare in photographs that it is not necessarily a problem. In most photographs, the flare from the lens is greater than that from sensor blooming.

Another defect noticeable in isolated highlights—or at least along strong luminosity edges—is chromatic aberration. There are two kinds, axial and lateral, and in modern lenses it is the lateral aberration that tends to be the culprit. The role played in this by sensor blooming (see box below) is disputed, and is probably tied to a different aberration known as "purple fringing." Lateral chromatic aberration shows itself as two opposed colors, usually red-cyan or blue-yellow,

SENSOR BLOOMING AND PURPLE FRINGING

Another detail from the Tokyo night shot, highly magnified, shows the effects of blooming, or flare, when highlights are over-exposed. Sensor blooming occurs when photosites fill up and the charge leaks to adjacent wells. The left image was shot at 1/3 sec and the center one at 2 sec. In the 2 sec exposure light is spilling over from the edges of the neon display. The right-hand image is the 1/3 sec exposure processed for an increase of nearly 3 stops to bring it to approximately the same brightness as the center. This creates a very noisy image with exaggerated fringing, but blooming is not noticeable to the same degree.

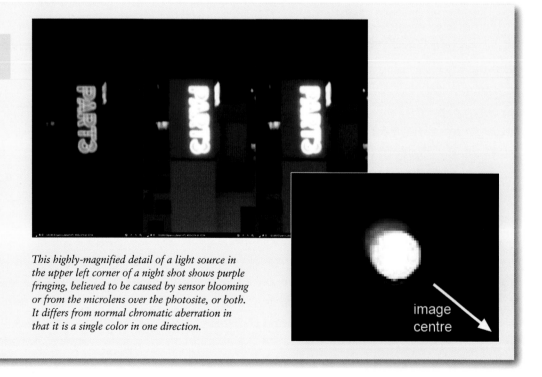

This highly-magnified detail of a light source in the upper left corner of a night shot shows purple fringing, believed to be caused by sensor blooming or from the microlens over the photosite, or both. It differs from normal chromatic aberration in that it is a single color in one direction.

image centre

and is increasingly common because of wide-range zooms, which are difficult for lens manufacturers to correct across the range. Also, every photographer is now a few clicks away from a magnified view of every image, so these things are simply noticed more. There are several solutions, as shown here, depending on the software. Most typical is a manual operation, moving a slider, and this works by expanding one channel relative to another. There is also defringing software that works on the edges themselves. A more automated solution is to use a pre-calculated lens module that corrects for the aberration in known lens-camera combinations, such as DxO Optics Pro.

Noise is one of the special new problems that arrived with digital photography. It is the visual equivalent of audible noise such as static hiss that degrades the quality of music. In a photograph it appears as a random pattern of pixels, usually bright and multi-colored, superimposed on the image. The comparison that is frequently made with grain in film is far too generous, as grain structure in an emulsion can contribute a gritty texture that is possible to like. Noone to my knowledge has ever made a case for digital noise being aesthetically pleasing. In terms of appearance (rather than cause), there is luminance noise (the random pattern of pixels varies from dark to light), chrominance noise (the pixels vary in hue), "dead" pixels (bright dots) and JPEG artifacts if you shoot JPEGs (blocks of 8×8 pixels can be prominent as these are used in the compression). Noise is a particular issue for lowlight photography because whether you increase the ISO for handheld shooting, or increase the exposure time for tripod-mounted shooting, noise will be created.

Chromatic aberration
A night view of Shibuya, Tokyo, shows lateral chromatic aberration from a wide-angle zoom. Different solutions are explored on page 13.

LIGHT ON THE SENSOR

Photoshop CS3's Raw converter offers the usual two-color sliders, which shift the channels, and in addition an even more useful defringer.

LensFix for Mac and PTLens for Windows have pre-calculated lens modules, although chromatic aberration needs to be adjusted manually by the user.

LOW LIGHT

DxO Optics Pro loads pre-calculated lens modules, which take care of the geometric distortion and the lateral chromatic aberration automatically.

A comparison of CA correction between software. From left to right, uncorrected, corrected in Photoshop ACR, corrected in DxO, corrected in PTLens, corrected in LensFix.

Photoshop ACR (uncorrected)

Photoshop ACR (corrected)

LensFix

PTLens

DxO Optics Pro

LIGHT ON THE SENSOR

DIGITAL NOISE

A simple comparison of noise at different camera settings. Noise is always most apparent in smooth areas that are dark, but above black. Practically, the major difference in noise comes from changing the ISO sensitivity. This sequence runs from the minimum ISO setting of 100 on a Nikon D200, to the maximum of 3200. A point to note is that in terms of appearance, these noise effects are exponential—meaning they set in quite late on the scale, but at the high end of ISO choices quickly become objectionable.

The second most common kind of noise is dark noise from long exposures, and here, at a one-minute exposure, the noise is much less of an issue with this sensor and this camera than the random noise from high ISO. There is an only-just-noticeable difference between the camera's dark-frame-subtraction process switched on and switched off. The temperature is critical, however. This sequence was shot at a reasonable room temperature of 21°C, but this kind of noise tends to double every 6°C to 8°C.

60 sec NR ON   *60 sec NR OFF*

Long Exposure comparison

ISO 100   *ISO 200*   *ISO 400*   *ISO 800*   *ISO 1600*

We will look at noise and noise reduction in detail in Chapters 2 and 3, but in practical terms it is essential to be thoroughly familiar with the appearance of noise as created by your camera in images that you typically shoot. Few people would disagree that noise is best avoided, but the amount of effort you go to in order to control it should depend on how important it is to you. Long-exposure noise can generally be taken care of quite well in the camera by selecting the noise-reduction option in the menu, but the immediate cause of most noise is setting a high ISO sensitivity. You may well find that for certain kinds of image, you can tolerate a higher ISO setting than you imagined. As an, important first step, make some tests at different ISO settings in a range of lowlight situations, and examine them side by side. At 100% magnification, you can expect to see increasing noise with higher ISO settings most obviously in smooth shadow areas. Decide for yourself at what setting it becomes objectionable. As noted earlier, on pages 16-17, you need to find an acceptable balance between the usefulness of a high ISO setting and the degree of noise.

There are several variables when it comes to making this decision. One is the medium that you normally use for displaying your images. If this is a print, then you should make tests using your preferred paper type. The appearance of noise will be different between a 100% screen view and a print. A related variable is the size at which the images will be used. A fully magnified print will obviously show more noise than a 640×480 pixel screen image posted on a website. A third variable is the kind of image. A reportage shot with visible noise is likely to be tolerated by more people than would be a still-life or landscape. Yet another variable is knowing how much you can expect to, or are willing to, reduce the noise later with software (the subject of pages 146-155).

Ultimately, when shooting you should be armed with enough information and judgment so that you can confidently select the appropriate ISO setting. You may, for instance, see hardly any difference in noise between shooting at ISO 100 (if your camera allows this sensitivity) and ISO 200, in which case the extra shooting speed carries no penalty. The ISO setting is one of several ways of achieving a certain shutter speed, and the others include supporting the camera, sacrificing depth of field by opening up the aperture, switching to a faster lens, and supporting the camera. Each carries some disadvantage, even if minor, so consider the ISO selection in this context. Maximizing shooting efficiency may mean altering the ISO frequently, and some cameras allow it to be changed by means of a dial, which is much faster than repeatedly going to the menu.

As well as technical matters of exposure, such as holding highlights and avoiding shadow noise, which are all the more critical with artificial light sources, you need to decide whether a scene should look dim rather than fully bright; in other words, the key of the shot. With a night image, this is perfectly expected—it would look strange otherwise—but there are many less obvious situations where there is room for interpretation. The example I've chosen here is deliberately not a clear-cut case; a Hakka communal dwelling in China, where the sensation inside the circular three-storey structure, open to the sky, was distinctly subdued.

THE CASE FOR LOWER KEY

For shots taken in low light to convey that impression, the key of the finally processed image needs to be lower than normal. This is entirely a matter of taste, but here, the darker of the two versions is more faithful to the original impression—something that only the photographer can decide. The histogram is always a good check—the bulk of the tones centered is a normal key, shifted to the left is low key.

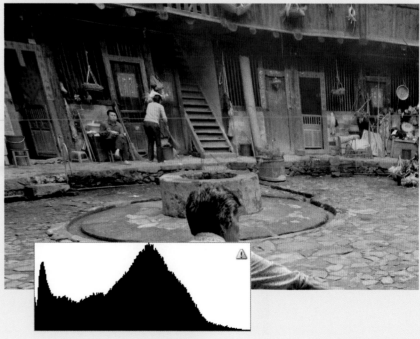

THRESHOLDS AND TRADEOFFS

In one important sense, lowlight photography is not just another situation, or just another themed area of photography. It carries with it a challenge; that in order to work in these lighting conditions you are forfeiting predictability. The lighting conditions themselves are never quite sufficient to allow the perfect camera settings, so not only are you close to reaching the shooting limits, but you will always have to make technical compromises. If you sacrifice shutter speed, you run the risk of motion blur or camera blur. You can trade this against a number of other things, including aperture, noise from a higher ISO setting, lens focal length, viewpoint,

Lowlight photography sets several practical limits to capturing a clean, sharp image, based on shutter speed, aperture, and noise.

the moment of shooting and more besides. The list of choices go on, and are always specific to the scene in front of you. The point I'm laboring here, because I think it worth a couple of pages, is that lowlight photography has built into it the idea of pushing the envelope. The reward, as just mentioned, is being able to work in, and capture an area of life, that was up until recently fairly restricted to photography. The price is a higher level of concentration on technical matters, and a higher failure rate, which simply takes some getting used to.

Photography as a whole is premised on there being enough light to work easily, and the norm is full daylight. There's no precise definition for this, but it goes from around 8a.m. to 5p.m. Not surprisingly, cameras and their sensors are designed for trouble-free operation in these conditions, meaning that the

Wide-angle, low light
The compromise in a shot like this, taken with an 18mm efl lens, is between depth of field, subject movement, and noise, affecting aperture, shutter speed, and ISO. Of the several possibilities, I chose f5.6 with careful focus, 1/10 sec and ISO 400. In other words, I favored low noise, and shot many frames to guarantee the final image.

FREEZING MOVEMENT

The following factors affect the shutter speed:

• How fast the subject is moving

• The angle of movement to the camera: head-on, side-on, or diagonal

• Distance from the camera

• Focal length of the lens

In addition, the following set limits to the speed that is actually possible:

• The need for good depth of field (from a smaller aperture)

• The amount of acceptable noise

• The amount of acceptable motion blur

• The amount and direction of light

• Size of reproduction or viewing of the final image

The limits of motion blur
Often, motion blur can be acceptable if limited in extent, provided that it leaves key parts of the image recognizable. Indeed, the movement, in this case of a Tibetan pilgrim, can bring life and energy to a shot.

sensor can operate at its lowest, cleanest sensitivity for highest image quality and yet still allow a choice of shutter speed and aperture. These in turn give you flexibility in capturing motion and in deciding on the appropriate depth of field. In order to shoot successfully in these more restricted conditions, you lose any flexibility. On the contrary, none of the settings are likely to be what you would really like.

Because lowlight photography is constrained by performance limits, shooting always involves compromise, adjusting the camera settings to sacrifice one technical function in favour of another. These are the tradeoffs, and it's easy to see them as a permanent set of difficulties, but practically it usually works better to treat them more positively, as ways of getting you closer to images that are only recently possible.

In a wider sense, of course, all good photography pushes limits of one kind or another. Whether these are creative limits, like composition, or technical limits (as in low light) is not a great distinction, because each affects the other. Pushing the technical limits of shutter speed and aperture, and the ability to hand-hold steadily and choose the right settings for the situation, ultimately contributes to the creative success of an image. At this edge of technical acceptability there are bound to be failures and disappointments, perhaps many for each shot, which that makes this edge-pushing worthwhile. If you feel this, and are happy living with the uncertainty, lowlight photography has a permanent level of excitement.

Using motion blur deliberately
Turning the problem around creates new opportunities. In this situation, of priests at prayer in a Shinto shrine, the camera was mounted on a tripod and the shot was framed to include a significant part of the setting (which remains sharp), while the white-clad figures flow insubstantially in a one-second exposure.

THE RANGE OF LIGHT SOURCES

By definition, the quantity of light is always much less than the reference standard for photography and human vision alike—the sun. Midday sunlight, clear and unfiltered by clouds or haze, produces around 100,000 to 130,000 lux (see box). The lighting in a typical office is probably between 200 and 400 lux, so the difference between the two in practical photographic terms is about EV 7 or 8. Put even more practically, at ISO 100 a typical setting for bright midday would be 1/125 sec at *f*16, while in an office you would be shooting at, say, 1/15 to 1/30 sec at *f*2.8 at the same level of sensitivity.

Lowlight photography extends into interiors and night scenes, and so meets the widest variety of artificial lighting possible, each with its own characteristics of output, color and frequency.

One consequence of this is that in low light there is no typical, easily predictable setting. Levels vary hugely, as the table opposite shows. Not only this, but the illumination from all local light sources, as we'll see on the following pages, tends to be uneven. The illumination fades rapidly with distance from each lamp. The most common artificial light sources, which we'll examine in detail in chapter 2, are vapor discharge lamps of several varieties, fluorescent lamps, and incandescent lamps. Many interiors and nighttime exteriors have a mix of these light sources, which under some circumstances can create interesting and attractive visual effects, but which can also be a headache for tonal and color balance.

Light sources vary not only in intensity but in the color of the light they emit. The human eye manages to accommodate these differences so well that for the most part we are unaware of any major difference, other than perhaps a "warm" appearance from incandescent lighting and a slightly "cool" effect from the kind of fluorescent lamps typical in super-markets and vapor discharge lamps in a stadium or warehouse. However, the camera's sensor, as with film, captures the true emission, unfiltered by our complex eye-brain processing.

Flame
Flame is the basic, original artificial light source, and still features occasionally in lowlight photographic situations

Tungsten
The range of tungsten lamps for domestic use is typically between 40 and 100 watts, and in color temperature between 2750 K (40 watts) and 2850 K (100 to 150 watts). However, fittings such as lampshades reduce and diffuse this output, and introduce color shifts.

CFLs

CFLs (Compact Fluorescent Lamps) are becoming increasingly common in domestic interiors for their efficiency and low heat output. However, they cause difficulties in color rendering in photography, because they lack a full spectrum.

Flourescent

Fluorescent and vapor discharge lamps have discontinuous spectra, and while the human eye accommodates for this quite easily, camera sensors and film record color shifts that are sometimes strong, and often towards green.

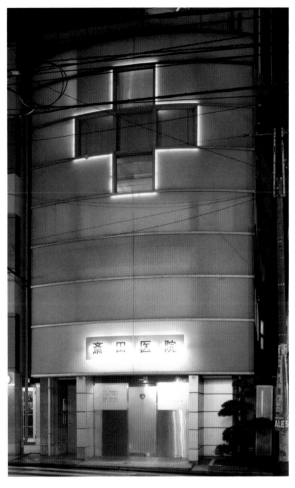

LOWLIGHT LEVELS

The fundamental measurement unit of scene brightness is the lux. This is one lumen per square meter, and measures the amount of light falling on a scene. It has nothing to do with the light reflected from surfaces, takes no account of what is in the scene, and is akin to an incident light reading (as taken with a handheld meter). The unit more familiar to photographers is EV, or Exposure Value, and the values given here relate to surfaces in the scene, and assume average reflectivity. EV varies according to the sensitivity to which the camera is set, and the single figures given here assume ISO 100. Doubling the ISO would increase the EV by 1. EV can also be expressed more practically as a combination of shutter speed and aperture, and the examples given here are only one of many combinations. Thus, EV 7 at ISO 100 could be 1/15 sec at *f*2.8, or 1/30 sec at *f*2, or 1 sec at *f*11, for example.

Lighting situation	Lux (light falling on scene)	EV (Exposure Value) at ISO 100	Typical speed & aperture at ISO 100
Television studio	1,000	EV 9	1/60 sec *f*2.8
Indoor office	200 to 400	EV 7 – 8	1/15 - 1/30 sec *f*2.8
Dark, overcast	100	EV 5 – 6	1/4 -1/8 sec *f*2.8
Twilight	10	EV 2	2 sec *f*2.8
Deep twilight	1	EV -1.3	20 sec *f*2.8
Average full moon	0.25	EV -3	1 min *f*2.8
Average quarter moon	0.025	EV -6.5	12min *f*2.8

CONTRAST ISSUES

The illumination from any light source falls off with distance, which is fairly obvious if you think of a flashlight aimed out into the dark, or the way a room looks when only one table lamp is switched on. In normal daylight photography this is not a consideration, because of the great distance of the sun. Any difference between the sunlight reaching a mountain top and that at sea level is insignificant compared with the 93 million miles between the sun and earth. Photography by any kind of artificial lighting, which covers the majority of most peoples' lowlight shooting, has to deal with a very different distribution of illumination.

The light fall-off from a point source of light, such as a bare bulb, follows a simple law. It fades in inverse proportion to the square of the distance, hence the name the Inverse Square Law. So, for example, the illumination two meters away from a lamp is four times less than at one meter ($1 \times 1m = 1$, $2 \times 2m = 4$). Put more pragmatically, light falls off rapidly, and the result in city streets at night and interiors with mainly spotlighting, such as restaurants and clubs, is a lighting

Local light sources, meaning anything other than the sun, have the important characteristic of creating pools of light, bringing opportunities for drama but also problems of contrast.

Iban Man
Because light sources in lowlight situations tend to be local, contrast is often high and shadows deep, as in this image of an Iban man resting after work under a small window.

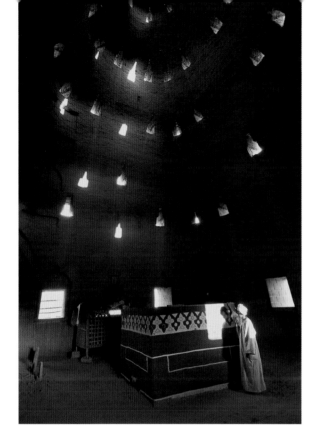

High contrast

Sunlight streaming through an array of small triangular openings in a Sudanese tomb create an unusual and attractive effect. When contrast is very high, yet the darker areas dominate the best strategy is to let the highlights go.

BALANCING MIXED LIGHT

To the eye, a living space like this, partly lit by subdued daylight, and with white walls helping to even out the illumination, appears reasonably balanced. A photograph, however, reveals the concentrated high illumination from spotlights and lamps, which tend to burn out in the image. New techniques of blending a dark and a light exposure, however (see page 194), achieve a more balanced effect that is truer to our visual impression.

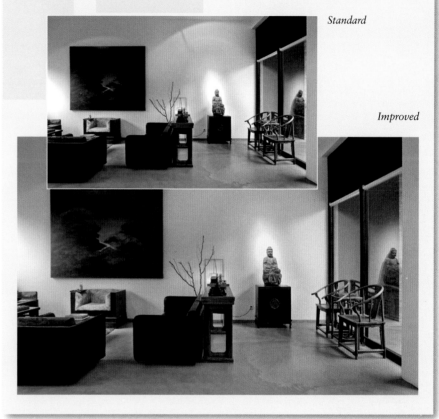

Standard

Improved

pattern of pools of light surrounded by shadows. More lights add to the complication of the lighting design, and broad area lights such as diffuse concealed ceiling lighting, lessen the fall-off. The net result is more often than not a high degree of local contrast.

This is one of the most basic technical issues in lowlight photography, and many of the techniques in this book are aimed at dealing with it. High contrast means not only that the dynamic range of a scene may be beyond the ability of the sensor to capture it in one exposure, but that there are likely to be significant shadow areas where detail is lost and where there is visible noise. The situation is made even more difficult when light sources themselves appear in shot—street lamps, downlighters set into ceilings, neon display advertising, and similar. The traditional ways of dealing with bright pools of light and dark shadows focus on composition and viewpoint, such as moving the camera to hide a bright spotlight. Composition can also make use of the chiaroscuro effect of light and shade, and to

an extent some area or areas of dense shadow and lost, burnt-out highlight can be acceptable in the image.

Nevertheless, digital techniques, both in capture and post-production, offer another way out of this situation, by effectively increasing the dynamic range. A relatively new technique is HDR Imaging, in which a sequence of exposures is captured, then compressed into a single image file that covers a very wide dynamic range. Shooting Raw also potentially offers a higher dynamic range, although it depends on the exposure at capture as a completely clipped highlight is not recoverable. Either way, post-production offers an increasing array of smart techniques for doing the two things that were virtually impossible on film—restoring highlights and opening up shadows.

RESTORING HIGHLIGHTS

In order of priority for human perception, the mid-tones of an image are naturally the most important, but they are followed closely by highlights, with shadows in last place. Apart from light sources themselves, such as lamps, which are expected to be super-white, we tend to sense something wrong in an image where the highlights are well over-exposed. Dense shadows without features are more easily tolerated. This, more than anything, is the basic rationale for exposing to hold the highlights.

Quite apart from special techniques such as bracketing exposures, the format you choose and the software you use can perform near-miracles in recovering highlights in a high-contrast scene.

Nevertheless, there is a range of post-production techniques for recovering detail in highlight areas. All are premised on there being some detail captured. As we've seen, a completely blown highlight (255, 255, 255 in RGB) is simply empty space in the image. Once a photosite has filled up completely, there is no recovery possible. If one channel has blown, and sometimes even if two channels have blown, there is some recovery possible in Raw, but this is the limit.

The Raw converter is indeed the place to begin highlight recovery if you are shooting this format. The more advanced image-editors have algorithms for attempting to reconstruct image detail from the remaining channel or channels. In Photoshop CS3, for example, the Raw converter has a specific Recovery slider for this. Dragging it all the way to 100% will also affect midtone areas, but these can be pulled back with either or both the Fill and Brightness controls.

With TIFFs and JPEGs, the most basic technique is an adjustment in Curves. For maximum control first sample the areas of highlight that you want to alter, in order to define exactly which section of the curve to drag. Anchoring other parts of the tonal range by selecting points on the curve below and even above this section will help to constrain the effect. However, curve adjustments tend to carry some unwanted side-effects, like lowering contrast. Some recent methods are starting to make Curves look primitive.

These methods of altering tonal range take account of the spatial location of each pixel, and are a form of local operator. Probably the best-known is Photoshop's Shadows/Highlights control. This, as do other similar methods, alters local contrast within a certain radius of each pixel. The radius can be adjusted in the dialog window, as can the strength of the darkening or lightening and the range of tones covered. For highlight recovery, it is the second group of sliders in the Shadows/Highlights dialog window that are effective. Even so, extreme settings produce unrealistic results.

Yet another technique for highlight recovery is to first isolate the lighter areas of the image. From Photoshop's Lab Color mode you can easily make a luminosity mask, effectively selecting the lightest 50% of pixels in an image. In the Channels palette, with the Lightness channel active, click on the lower left dotted circle. The pop-up description is "Load channel as selection." In other words, the tones of the image are being made into a mask, and the result is an instant selection of the lightest half of the image. To this selection you can then apply any of a number of processes, including Curves, Levels, Shadows/Highlights, and even the low-intensity/high-radius USM technique described on the following pages.

THE LIMITS OF THE RAW ADVANTAGE

Shooting JPEG has 256 shades per channel (red, green, and blue), which the computer describes as incremental values from 0-255. That's because 255 is expressed as 11111111 in binary, the highest number you can fit into eight bits. Shooting in 12-bits dramatically increases this to 4096 possible values, allowing for greater accuracy. Nevertheless if all the channels are fully exposed it doesn't matter whether the maximum value is 255 or 4095, they still represent 100%, or pure white.

FLAMES

In this shot of a firecrackers being thrown into a furnace in a Chinese temple, the flames are well over-exposed, but recovery of sorts is possible.

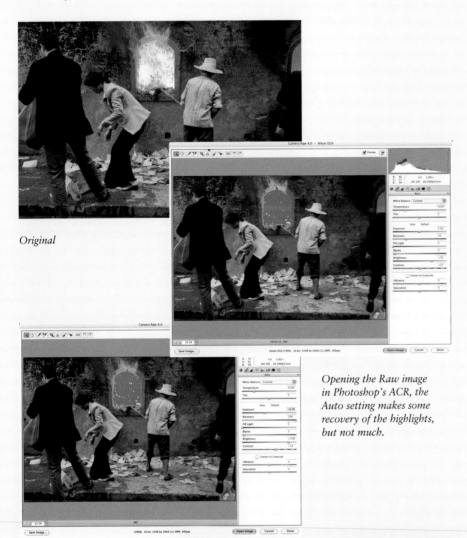

Original

In Shadows/Highlights, Shadows are turned off, as we only want to recover the highlights. The first step is to find the tonal width that covers all the flames in the furnace opening. To do this, the Highlights amount is set to maximum, and the Tonal Width slider moved around to find the best effect. The Radius slider is also moved to find the most pleasing effect.

Opening the Raw image in Photoshop's ACR, the Auto setting makes some recovery of the highlights, but not much.

The Highlights Amount is then adjusted for best effect.

Extra manual recovery delivers a slight improvement, achieved by increasing recovery to the maximum, decreasing exposure and increasing Brightness.

The resulting TIFF is the starting point for more operations in post-processing.

Camera Raw 4.0 – Nikon D2X

Preview

R: 39
G: 34
B: 31

f/4   1/90 s
ISO 160   18-200@31mm

Basic

White Balance: Custom

Temperature   4200
Tint   0

Auto   Default

Exposure   -2.20
Recovery   100
Fill Light   0
Blacks   3
Brightness   +109
Contrast

Convert

Vibrance
Saturation

Further recovery is possible by going back to the Raw conversion and reducing the exposure severely, until no highlight clipping is evident. Of course, this also darkens the rest of the scene.

22.1%   18702.24 . NEF

Adobe RGB (1998); 16 bit; 4288 by 2848 (12.2MP); 300ppi

Save Image...   Open Image   Can

Normal   Opacity 100%

Lock: 100%

Layer 1

Background

fx

: Custom

Layer Style

Blending Options
General Blending

Blend Mode: Normal

Opacity: 100 %

Advanced Blending

Fill Opacity: 100 %
Channels: ☑ R ☑ G ☑ B
Knockout: None

☐ Blend Interior Effects as Group
☑ Blend Clipped Layers as Group
☑ Transparency Shapes Layer
☐ Layer Mask Hides Effects
☐ Vector Mask Hides Effect

Blend If: Gray

This Layer: 129 / 216   255

Underlying Layer: 0   255

☐ Outer Glow
☐ Inner Glow
☐ Bevel and Emboss
  ☐ Contour
  ☐ Texture
☐ Satin
☐ Color Overlay
☐ Gradient Overlay
☐ Pattern Overlay
☐ Stroke

OK
Cancel
New Style...
☑ Preview

This darker version of the image is copied and pasted as a layer, and this is then blended for the flame highlights, using Blending Options. This brings back a great deal of information, although now there is a lack of contrast within the flames area.

LOW LIGHT

24

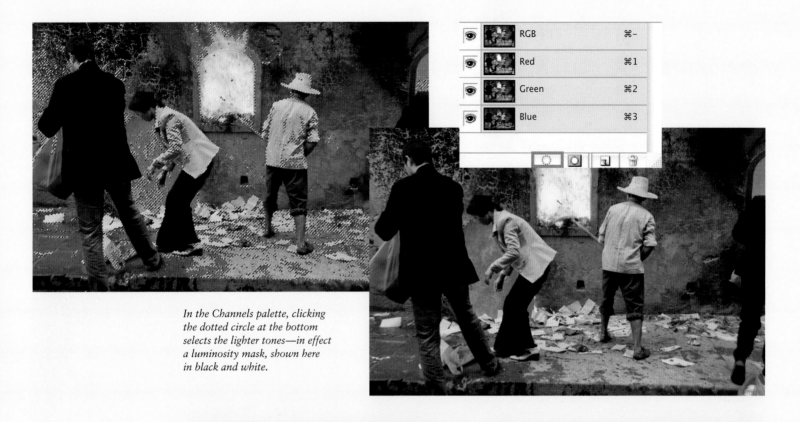

		RGB	⌘~
		Red	⌘1
		Green	⌘2
		Blue	⌘3

In the Channels palette, clicking the dotted circle at the bottom selects the lighter tones—in effect a luminosity mask, shown here in black and white.

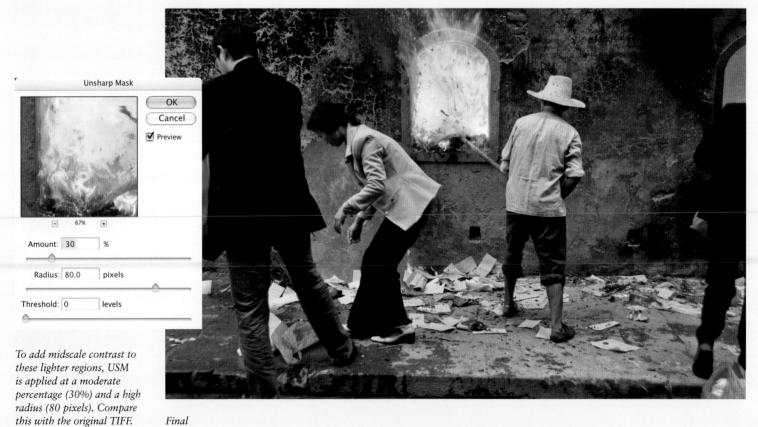

Unsharp Mask

OK

Cancel

☑ Preview

− 67% +

Amount: 30 %

Radius: 80.0 pixels

Threshold: 0 levels

To add midscale contrast to these lighter regions, USM is applied at a moderate percentage (30%) and a high radius (80 pixels). Compare this with the original TIFF.

Final

REVEALING SHADOWS

Just as highlights can be recovered in post-production, so shadows can be opened up to reveal information that appears lost and dense at first glance.

As with highlight recovery, if your exposure has been made for the midtones, as is usual, there will often be a need to lighten the shadows in a high-contrast image. As just explained, dense shadows are perceptually more acceptable than washed-out highlights. At the same time, however, there is usually more that can be recovered, for the reason that there are usually some photons of light that have entered even the darkest photosite on the sensor. Practically, this means that it is usually easier in most images to pull more detail out of shadows than out of highlights. There is an important limitation, however, which is that the most noise is in the shadow areas (see pages 142), and any enhancement of shadow detail will exaggerate this noise. In the darkest areas, the signal-to-noise ratio may be so low as to mark the limits of useful image. So, any shadow recovery technique usually benefits from noise reduction as well (see pages 146-155).

The techniques are similar (though in reverse procedure) to those for highlight recovery, beginning with the Raw converter. In Photoshop CS3, the relevant slider is Fill. Understandably, it has a slight flattening effect on the dark-to-mid-tones, and may benefit from some contrast enhancement. The upper set of sliders in Photoshop's Shadows/Highlights control work as the Highlights do (see page 24). And, just as the luminosity mask isolates the lighter pixels in an image, inverting the selection once this has been done allows you to operate on the darker 50% of the image. Another way of thinking about this under-explained feature is that of a grayscale version of the image used as a mask.

Finally, it's worth mentioning in this context another local contrast enhancement technique that is really an unintended by-product of sharpening. This extremely useful technique is applied through the standard sharpening method known as unsharp mask (USM). While seemingly different in purpose, sharpening and local contrast enhancement are very closely related. Both depend on creating a soft mask, across which the contrast is increased. In USM, the contrast increase is on a very small scale—often a radius no more than one pixel—but quite strong, so that edges become more pronounced. In local contrast enhancement, the settings are reversed, with a very large radius, often as much as 100 pixels, but a small amount. The effect is larger scale transitions but without altering the global contrast of the image, and typically this is fairly subtle. In both cases, some pixels cross over each other in the histogram, making this completely different from a curves-based adjustment. The latter, one form or another of an S-curve, is a truly global adjustment.

Away from Photoshop, other image-editing software offers alternative techniques for opening up shadow areas, generally through either lightening a selected area or by means of tone-mapping and accentuating local contrast. The two programs featured here are both aimed at photographers in the sense that they deliberately avoid the Photoshop way of working. In different ways, they attempt to be both intuitive and automated, so as to speed up processing decisions. In the course of doing this, many of the arcane parameter sliders and tools common in Photoshop are concealed, or at least pushed into the background. This applies to shadow control as much as other procedures. DxO Optics Pro has very little showing in its controls that

MID-SCALE LOCAL CONTRAST ENHANCEMENT

Experiment with different settings of an Unsharp Mask filter to achieve clearer-looking shadow detail (without any sharpening). A good starting point is Amount 20%, Radius 60, Threshold 0, but much depends on the size of the image and the subtleties of the effect.

RAW SHADOW RECOVERY

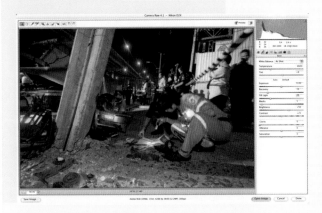

Photoshop ACR on Default

Photoshop ACR with Fill Light at 25

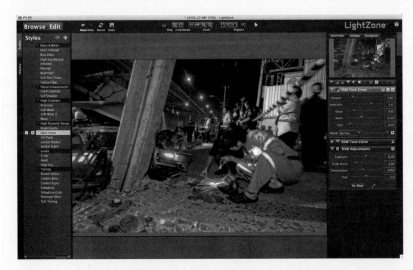

LightZone in Dark Scene Style, with the tonemapping sliders at default.

LightZone offers another option, Relight, which performs a similar procedure to DxO.

Before

Relit

Original

DxO uses the reverse option of Preserve shadows, which holds them dark. Without the option ticked, they receive tonemapping to open them up.

DxO Open Shadows

DxO Preserve Shadows

appears to be specifically aimed at opening up shadows, but the algorithms are there nevertheless. They are included in DxO Lighting tools, and the principle they use is segmentation, in which the image is analyzed for different ranges of luminance values, and these are then each treated slightly differently.

Shadow areas are generally given an increase in lightness and the tone curve slope. The choices Slight, Medium, and Strong then apply these, as well as other automatic adjustments, to different strengths accordingly. In addition, unchecking the Preserve Shadows checkbox opens them up even more, at the slight risk of a loss of naturalness.

LightZone offers more than one method of opening up shadows specifically. One is the Relight tool, which uses tone-mapping techniques similar to those seen in high dynamic range software to lighten shadow areas while maintaining the local contrast in the image (and the reverse for highlights).

Another is LightZone's basic Zone System approach to tonal adjustment, whereby a zone can be selected and dragged up or down in the scale to lighten or darken just those values. Yet another option is the distinct High dynamic range/Dark scene "style," one of a number of presets that opens up a tool giving options for adjusting shadows.

SHADOWS AND HIGHLIGHTS

Photoshop's post-processing option applies tonemapping selectively to darker and lighter areas.

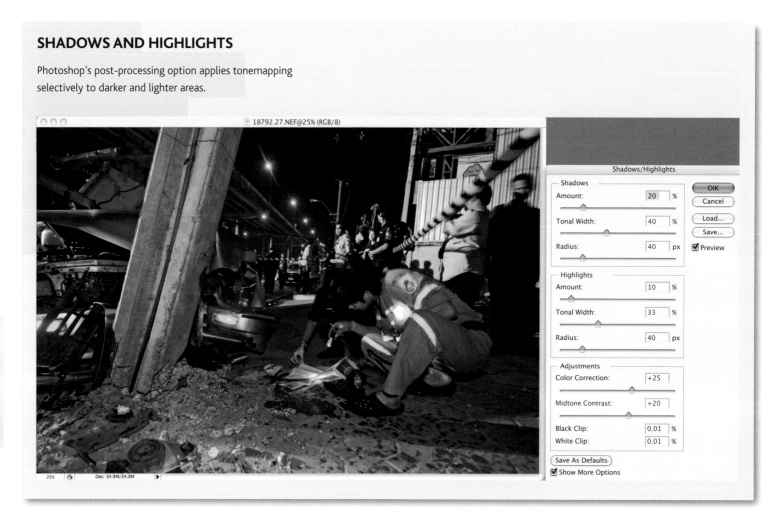

LOW LIGHT

SUBTLE RECOVERY WITH A LUMINOSITY MASK

This very gentle effect is achieved by first creating an inverted Luminosity mask, and then applying USM at low intensity and high radius.

Original

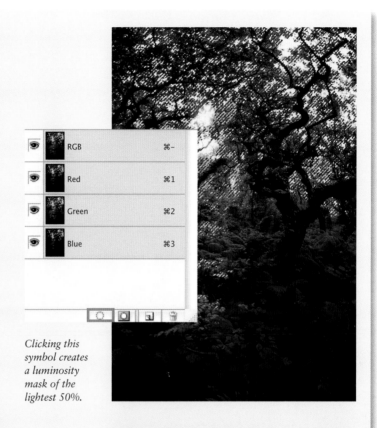

Clicking this symbol creates a luminosity mask of the lightest 50%.

Invert the selection to select the darkest 50% of the image.

USM applied to subtly add contrast to the shadows only.

SHADOW REALISM

O ver the last four pages we looked at a number of powerful post-production tools for recovering lost detail and enhancing limited detail at either end of the tonal scale. Because of the nature of lowlight photography and its typical situations, shadows play an very large part in the image. The efficiency of image-editing software in pulling detail out of shadows makes it tempting to use aggressively, but this carries some dangers. One obvious problem is the enhancement of noise. Even when noise is fairly evenly distributed across an image it is not particularly attractive. When it is concentrated very noticeably and patchily in the shadow areas, it is even worse.

Digital post-production now has such successful tools for opening up shadow areas that it has become essential to exercise careful photographic judgment to avoid unrealistic, over-bright results.

But beyond this, there is the more subjective issue of what looks right in an image. This is impossible to quantify, because it varies from viewer to viewer, and is affected not only by what we consider to be the normal, realistic appearance of a scene, but also by the way we have become accustomed to seeing photographs. In a sense, shadow recovery techniques are a small, but important part, of the much bigger issue of tone-mapping high dynamic range images. The effect that shadow recocery has is the appearance of more visual information, but not necessarily a more truthful, convincing, or even pleasing image. The sequence of image adjustments shown here make this obvious. As the recovery procedure is applied more intensely, the shadow areas throw up more and more detail, but at a certain point they begin to look false. Exactly which step looks false to you is a matter of personal judgment, but it has become one of the most common and glaring "faults" seen in today's digital image processing, especially with lowlight pictures.

JUDGING THE EXTENT OF TONEMAPPING

Using Photoshop's Shadows/Highlights for shadow recovery only, this series of different amounts shows that while increasing the amount of opening up shadows obviously reveals more and more detail, at a certain point the image looks artificial and lacking in what we would consider traditional photographic qualities. Overly aggressive use of this tool is a common mistake.

Original

Shadows / Highlights

Shadows
Amount: 10 %
Tonal Width: 50 %
Radius: 40 px

Highlights
Amount: 0 %
Tonal Width: 0 %
Radius: 40 px

Adjustments
Color Correction: 0 %
Midtone Contrast: 0 %
Black Clip: 0.01 %
White Clip: 0.01 %

OK
Cancel
Load...
Save...
☑ Preview

Save As Defaults
☑ Show More Options

Shadows/ Highlights

Shadows
Amount: 20 %
Tonal Width: 50 %
Radius: 40 px

Highlights
Amount: 0 %
Tonal Width: 0 %
Radius: 40 px

Adjustments
Color Correction: 0 %
Midtone Contrast: 0 %
Black Clip: 0.01 %
White Clip: 0.01 %

OK
Cancel
Load...
Save...
☑ Preview

Save As Defaults
☑ Show More Options

Shadows/Highlights

Shadows
Amount: 40 %
Tonal Width: 50 %
Radius: 40 px

Highlights
Amount: 10 %
Tonal Width: 33 %
Radius: 40 px

Adjustments
Color Correction: 0 %
Midtone Contrast: 0 %
Black Clip: 0.01 %
White Clip: 0.01 %

OK
Cancel
Load...
Save...
☑ Preview

Save As Defaults
☑ Show More Options

Shadows/Highlights

Shadows
Amount: 80 %
Tonal Width: 50 %
Radius: 40 px

Highlights
Amount: 10 %
Tonal Width: 33 %
Radius: 40 px

Adjustments
Color Correction: 0 %
Midtone Contrast: 0 %
Black Clip: 0.01 %
White Clip: 0.01 %

OK
Cancel
Load...
Save...
☑ Preview

Save As Defaults
☑ Show More Options

SHADOW REALISM

COLOR TEMPERATURE

Color temperature is arguably more important in lowlight photography than in any other, because the range of light sources you are likely to encounter vary widely on this scale. First though, with apologies to all those people who know this already, a brief primer on the color temperature scale, and the reasons why it has a place in photography. It all starts with the sun, which is the reference standard in several ways for human vision. Its light, at least when it is high in the sky, is what we call white. As this light is created by burning—incandescent, in other words—there is an exact correlation between temperature and "whiteness." The unit of temperature used is the Kelvin, which is basically similar to Celsius/Centigrade but starts at absolute zero (-273°C). Something burning at a lower temperature than the sun, such as a candle, produces a redder light. Something burning at a higher temperature (few things on Earth practically, but a hotter star for example) produces a light that is more blue. When most artificial lighting was incandescent—tungsten lamps—it made sense to use temperature as a color scale, from red through orange, amber, straw and white to increasing blue.

It makes less sense now that artificial lighting is increasingly dominated by fluorescent, vapor discharge and even LED lamps, but because photography has

The wide range of light sources that are a characteristic of lowlight photography does not fit precisely to the standard scale of color temperature, but the concept of correlated color temperature makes them manageable.

Choosing a balance
A typical domestic tungsten lamp has a color temperature of around 2800 K, while cool daylight is around 6000 K. The sequence here shows the same image balanced for each of these extremes and a compromise middle position.

Compromise

Balanced for outside

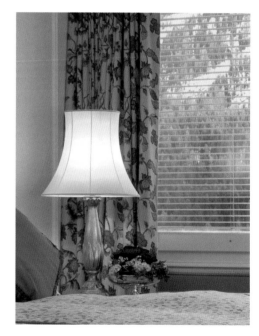

Balanced for inside

grown up using color temperature and Kelvin, these new light sources are made to fit into it the existing system. More accurately, they lie on a correlated color temperature scale.

The diagram shows what fits where. To be completely accurate, only incandescence really belongs on this scale, meaning the sun, an incandescent lamp such as tungsten or quartz-halogen, and a flame from a candle or a fireplace. Even the reddishness of the sun at sunset and sunrise, and the blue of the sky, are not strictly speaking on the scale, although they appear to fit very well. They are caused by the scattering of short wavelengths of light. Fluorescent and vapor discharge lamps only just fit at best, as they emit light by very different means, and they certainly need additional hue correction. To say that a typical fluorescent lamp has a color temperature of 4200 K, as does my camera instruction manual, is quite misleading and only partly useful.

Beware of confusing the natural, visual way of describing this kind of color shift with the real color temperature scale. To the eye, the lower color temperatures associated with flames and sunsets are "warm," while the higher color temperatures that make evening skies and open shade look bluish are what most people call "cool."

Sunlight
Sunset colors are created by refraction and scattering, and here cover the apparent range from about 3500 K to less than 1500 K. The actual color temperature of the sun's disc is under 6000 K.

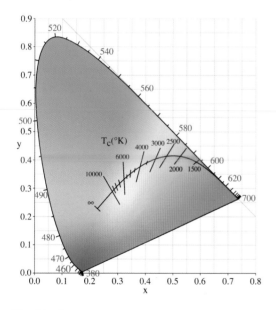

Planckian Locus
The color temperature scale plotted on a CIE 1931 x, y chromaticity space.

Candlelight
A candle flame emits at around 2000 K. In this image, the central flame seen through the glass and wine is clipped to white by the exposure, but the white tablecloth reveals the choice of White Balance in the Raw conversion—at 3100 K.

BLACK BODY AND COLOR TEMPERATURE

Accurate measurement of color temperature must be independent of the actual material being burned, as its ingredients could contribute to the color. For this reason, color temperature assumes a theoretical substance that is completely inert and does not burn away. It simply glows, and is called a "black body radiator."

WHITE BALANCE AND HUE

White balance in digital photography, as its name suggests, is the procedure for adjusting/correcting the overall color cast of lighting on a scene. The principle is that by identifying areas that should be white in the image, then making adjustments so that they appear true white without a color cast, the color of the light falling on all other areas of the picture will also be neutralized. The obvious place to do this is in the camera as soon as the image has been captured, and is practical because the color component of the image needs to be calculated in any case. As we saw on pages 21-25, the raw capture is of tonal values only—effectively a monochrome image—and the color is sensed by filtering these values, pixel by pixel, through a mosaic of red, green and blue. This mosaic, the Bayer array, has to be interpolated from neighboring pixels. It is relatively straightforward to bias this interpolation towards different color shifts. Naturally, this is more important in lowlight photography because of the wide range of possible light sources. Full, bright daylight varies very little when compared to artificial light sources.

This could actually be done in any number of ways, but because photography has grown up with color temperature, this is the scale used in all cameras.

Managing and editing the many different color casts can be tackled both in-camera and in post-production, particularly if you shoot in Raw, and this does not always mean neutralizing them.

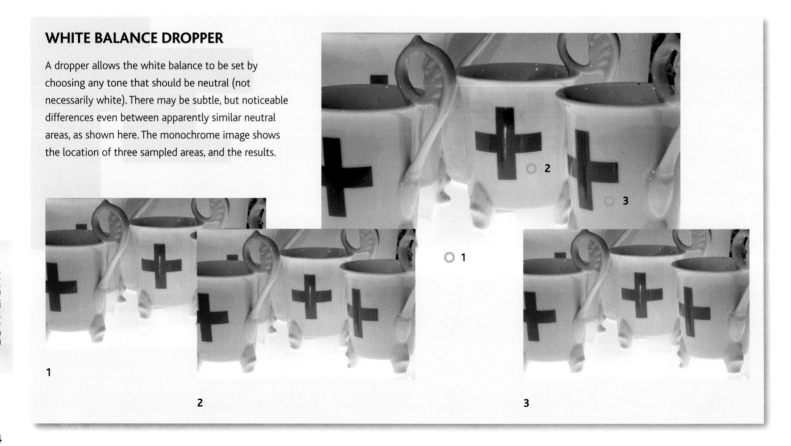

WHITE BALANCE DROPPER

A dropper allows the white balance to be set by choosing any tone that should be neutral (not necessarily white). There may be subtle, but noticeable differences even between apparently similar neutral areas, as shown here. The monochrome image shows the location of three sampled areas, and the results.

2

3

1

1

2

3

WHITE BALANCE SETTINGS

The white balance settings in the camera menu and, for Raw images, in a Raw converter, adjust color temperature and hue. These four versions, of white crockery set on a white Plexiglas display unit lit from beneath by unknown fluorescent lamps, are camera presets. They are accessible to a Raw converter if the image was shot, as here, in Raw format.

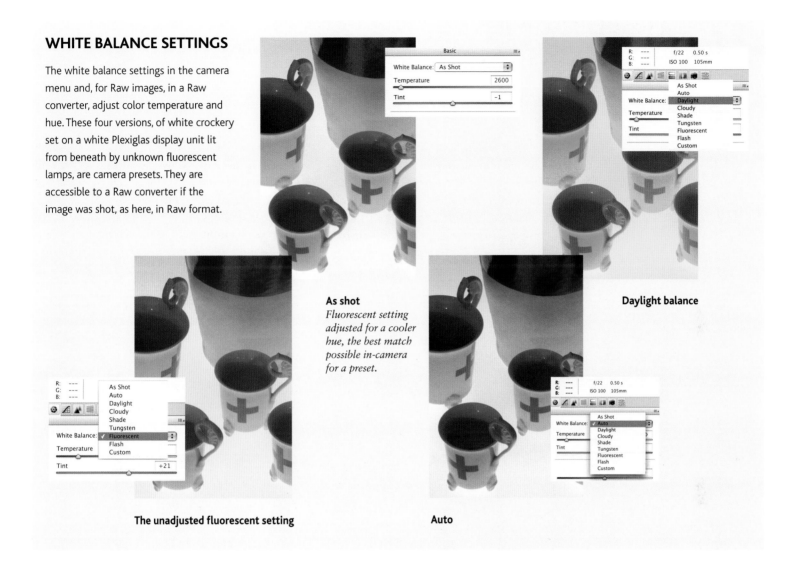

As shot
Fluorescent setting adjusted for a cooler hue, the best match possible in-camera for a preset.

Daylight balance

The unadjusted fluorescent setting

Auto

However, as we just saw, many light sources lack a continuous spectrum, and technically they do not really fit onto the scale of color temperature as measured in degrees Kelvin. But, because color temperature is such a familiar and convenient concept, they are made to fit approximately. This explains, as we'll see on pages 48-49, why the camera menu choices for fluorescent lighting frequently appear not quite right. Most good digital cameras also offer some adjustment to each white balance choice. This can be to raise or lower the color temperature a little, or to shift the colors around the color circle slightly. Check the camera manual to familiarize yourself with the method used, as this varies by manufacturer.

Shooting Raw, which is strongly recommended for lowlight photography, makes the white balance set in the camera irrelevant, as you can choose the settings with absolutely no loss of quality on the computer during processing. Raw converters, of which there are many, give not only a scale of color temperature, but also of hue. This is basically a second color axis more or less perpendicular to the color temperature scale, and the two together give a huge amount of possibility when it comes to color adjustment.

Technically speaking, choosing or tweaking the appropriate white balance setting for a particular image means neutralizing the color cast—making corrections so that it appears as if pure white light is falling across the entire scene. However, slavishly following this is not guaranteed to produce the most pleasing results. Not only are color casts not bad, they often contribute very much to the final color image.

KEY CAMERA SETTINGS FOR LOW LIGHT

Cameras' menus vary widely, and use different terminology, but if you have a digital SLR to reasonable specifications, be conscious of all the following settings, and make sure you're familiar with their operation. In some cases you might even be able to alter preset buttons to reach these settings faster.

IMAGE QUALITY AND FORMAT

The arguments for shooting Raw are stronger than ever in lowlight shooting, not least because it allows some latitude for recovering highlights and shadows, and allows you to defer decisions about color temperature until later, when you process the images on the computer.

An essential checklist of settings on the camera menu makes a lowlight shooting session easier and more efficient, and avoids some specific problems such as noise.

WHITE BALANCE

The importance of this setting depends entirely on whether or not you shoot Raw. If you do, then it hardly matters what you set at the time of shooting, although most people prefer to have the image preview on the camera's LCD screen looking approximately correct. Opinions vary, but my default preference is Auto. If, on the other hand, you are for some reason shooting JPEG or TIFF, then constant attention to the choices in the White Balance menu is necessary. Even so, it is worth comparing the previews between the tailored choice for the kind of light source (such as "Incandescent" or "Fluorescent") and Auto.

CONTRAST

Low contrast is always safer, as it is easier to increase later in post-production than to recover lost highlights and shadows. Many lowlight situations feature high contrast, especially those with light sources in the frame. If shooting Raw, this does not matter, as contrast is applied after capture.

ISO SENSITIVITY

This is likely to be the key control during lowlight shooting that you will access and change regularly. For traditional photographers, especially those used to using the same film in different conditions, it can be difficult to get used to the flexibility offered by instantly switchable ISO settings, but this is one of digital photography's biggest boons. Some cameras also offer an automatic ISO option.

NOISE REDUCTION

Although the instructions for most cameras rarely go into great detail about noise-reduction processes, the one referred to in the camera menu is dark frame/fixed pattern noise of the kind experienced with long exposures. This is predictable, because it is independent of the subject, and so in-camera processing is ideal. Check the camera manual, but choosing to set noise reduction to "on" will not affect shooting at normal shutter speeds. It will kick in at a specified exposure time; again, check the camera manual to see what this is for your model. At exposure times longer than this threshold, processing time doubles, because the automatic procedure involves creating a "dark frame" of the same exposure time, then subtracting the noise pattern in this from the previously exposed image. If you make a 30 second exposure, for example, you can expect to have to wait a further 30 seconds before you can shoot again. See page 174 for more details on this. Better cameras may offer both "long exposure noise reduction" and "high ISO noise reduction."

BRACKETING

Some cameras offer auto bracketing, in which a burst of exposures gives frames under- and over-exposed in addition to the metered exposure. This consumes storage space on the card and takes extra time when shooting, but if you feel uncertain about the exposure setting in some situations, it can be a useful backup (and you can always delete the unwanted exposures later if you need to).

Exposure warning

These screens simulate the clipping warnings that would be visible on screen as the shot is captured at different exposures. The green area is the clipped highlight warning, but the remaining colors are displayed accurately.

Adjusting the Auto Exposure Braketing to the nearest third of a stop on a Canon menu.

DISPLAY CHOICES

Because many lowlight scenes contain bright local lights and pools of light, it is useful to know when these are being over-exposed. The most useful display for this is the highlight clipping warning, in which over-exposed areas (where the photosites have filled up to their maximum values) are superimposed with a flashing warning. Some people find this distracting, but it is also valuable. A histogram is also particularly useful in low lighting situations, not least because the LCD screen image looks relatively brighter when the surrounding light is low. The danger of this is that if you judge exposure simply by this appearance, the image is likely to be under-exposed. Viewing it on the LCD screen later in normal lighting is likely to deliver an unpleasant surprise.

Nikon D300 menu offering both Long Exposure Noise Reduction and High ISO Noise Reduction options.

The Sony α700 menu allows the user to set limits for the automatic ISO adjustment.

NATURAL LOW LIGHT

Low lighting conditions divide reasonably into those of daylight and those of artificial lighting. The normal maximum daylight is outdoors, in the middle of the day in clear weather. As we've already seen, this is in the order of 100,000 lux or more. While it's probably going too far to say that the manufacturers of cameras, lenses, film, and sensors assumes this to be the standard, what most people would call bright daylight is the ideal condition technically. This was the "sunny 16" rule, from the days when many photographers would estimate settings, and it holds that the usual exposure on a sunny day is 1 over the film/sensor speed at f16 (thus 1/100 at f16 at ISO 100).

Daylight reaches low levels for photography not only at the ends of the day, but also under heavy weather conditions, and indoors.

What counts as low natural light sets in when it becomes difficult to guarantee sharp images with a normal lens and low ISO sensitivity. In practice, this means when it becomes difficult to either hold the camera steady, or freeze a normally moving subject at maximum aperture without taking special precautions such as fitting an unusually fast lens. There is no exact point, but this is somewhere around several hundred lux. Even during full daylight hours, thick cloud cover, rain, snow, and storms can reduce light levels to this low level. However, all we are talking about here are the technical difficulties as weather conditions such as these can deliver expressive imagery. Essentially, this is extreme diffusion, and so with cloud

Haboob

A sudden sandstorm, a variety known as a haboob in this Sudanese part of the eastern Sahara. Engulfed in a sand front, the light levels plunge and the neutral white balance of what was a bright, sunny afternoon, shifts to red.

cover the color temperature is affected only a little. With something more unusual, like a sandstorm, the color can shift radically, as the example on the left illustrates.

Natural light levels are also reduced by shade of one kind or another. Woodland in particular furnishes these conditions, especially on a small scale, and when the sky is clear there is likely to be a significant color temperature shift (higher, therefore bluer) as the shade is illuminated by the blue sky. A more common kind of shade is indoors, when the illumination during daylight hours is usually through windows. The age and architectural style of the building, together with the style of interior design, has a controlling influence here, but the major factor is the window area.

Outdoors, it is the ends of the day that create the main conditions for low light photography. Light changes quickly in both quantity and quality around sunrise and sunset, and while these two times of day may be indistinguishable to someone viewing the final photograph, they call for different shooting techniques to the middle of the day. The point at which the first and last sunlight of the day becomes a "lowlight" situation is highly variable, and generally hinges on the

Cloudy dawn
First light over an Andean town, with heavy weather and low clouds contributing to very low light levels (the building lights still dominate).

In cloud
Stormy conditions at the summit of a volcano, typical enough in this area in Costa Rica to create a permanent cloud forest.

NATURAL LOW LIGHT

usual technical issues of shutter speed and aperture. Generally speaking, when you need to take precautions on camera shake and subject motion blur, you are taking a lowlight photograph. This depends on choice of subject, focal length of lens, and the depth of the scene, so becomes an issue when shooting away from the sun some time before it is for shots taken into the sun.

For photography, the two features that dominate this time of day are the sheer variety of lighting angle and the color. With the sun low in the sky, its light rakes horizontal surfaces, hence creating good textures on flat landscapes, and strikes vertical ones, like people and buildings, from one side only. When you factor in the choice of camera viewpoint by moving around a scene, these times of day offer the greatest variety of

lighting quality of any. Backlighting, frontal lighting, and all degrees of sidelighting are all there at one time. Above all, this is what makes the ends of the day so useful in photography.

Color also changes. For most of the day, the color temperature under a direct sun is a fairly constant 5200 K, or rather higher under cloud (up to around 6000 K). When the sun is close to the horizon, at around 20° elevation or less, the color temperature falls, and the light becomes more yellow-to-red. This warm-looking color cast is caused by atmospheric scattering. Particles in the atmosphere scatter the higher-energy, shorter wavelengths of sunlight, and as these are in the blue-to-violet end of the spectrum, what is left is more reddish. How red the light is

Merlin's Cave

The legendary Merlin, teacher of King Arthur, is reputed to have lived in this cave, under the Tintagel Castle which is situated on the rugged north coast of Cornwall. The only light source is that from the cave's entrance, so much of the light falls across the surfaces near there at an extreme angle, with the remainder stemming from a minimal reflection from the dark rocks.

Indoor light
This shot was taken in a well-lit artist's studio, but to capture it at f 8 nevertheless requires a shutter speed of 1/5 second.

Ansar prayer
Friday prayer at the Ansar Mosque in Omdurman. It is lit unevenly through the windows, with the additional complication of a strong paint color that affects the color balance.

depends on the composition of the atmosphere, as well as the amount of it the sun's rays are passing through. The sun appears at its reddest when right on the horizon because its rays are travelling through the greatest amount of low-altitude atmosphere. Expect between 3500 K and 4500 K on a fairly clear day.

Contrary to what many people expect, there is no general distinction in the quality of light between sunrise and sunset. In either case, the sun is low and casts long shadows, and the color temperature is low. However, for every specific location there is a very large difference, and making preparations to shoot differ greatly. The aspect of any major subject obviously matters — which way it faces — and there may be a number of idiosyncratic things to consider. Local weather may change, as in morning mist or late afternoon haze, activity in a scene is also often different. There tend to be fewer people around in the early morning, and if this is summer in high to mid latitudes, sunrise is well before most people are even awake. This is a key consideration if you want a view without people or traffic. In other words, to the viewer

Ends of the day
Although they may feel very different when, thanks in no small part to the different physical temperatures, the photographic conditions are similar at sunrise and sunset. The ground frost, however, would certainly not be present in the evening.

of a photograph taken with a low sun, there is no way of telling whether it was shot at the beginning or end of the day, other than by being familiar with the actual location. To the photographer, however, the distinction is extremely important for very local reasons.

Moving beyond the point when the sun is touching the horizon, dawn and dusk create special, shifting conditions that can often deliver lighting surprises. This is marvellous for exploration and also for adding image quality to scenes that might be mundane by day. When the sun is just below the horizon, there is a short period of faded light that may, under the right conditions, offer a different and unusual quality of light to a scene. This is at either end of the day, and the length of twilight is no precise thing. It depends on the latitude and season, and is shortest in the tropics and longest in high latitudes because of the angle at which the sun rises and sets. As a rule of thumb, twilight that is useful for photography is when the sun is between the horizon (taken as 0°) and about 15° below. This is a rather shorter period of time than for what most photographers would consider "golden light" when the sun is a little above the horizon. In any case, the cut-off point between twilight and night is a matter of personal judgment, and can depend on the weather.

If the sky is completely overcast, twilight is irrelevant and indistinguishable — the light simply fades or brightens. If, however, the weather is mainly clear, the color and tonal effects in the sky itself can be very attractive. Twilight without clouds creates a vertical gradation of tone and color as at no other time of the day, and is strongest in appearance in the direction of the light. Depending on the atmospheric conditions, the number of hues in the sky varies. The scale might

NATURAL LOW LIGHT

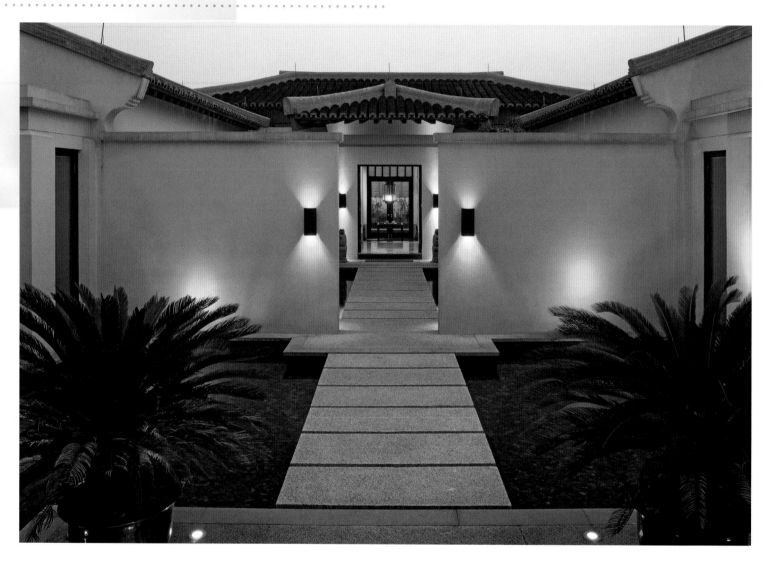

Formal garden at dusk
As dusk falls, the artificial lighting starts to compete with the natural light, which serves to add extra interest to this shot.

be from white to indigo, or from red through gray to blue. There is even the possibility of the "green flash," in which refraction of light in the atmosphere can momentarily color the tip of the sun green.

The most obvious use to make of twilight is as a backdrop to a silhouetted subject or sky-line, with the sky itself being in effect the main subject. In very clear weather, however, there may be enough color from the sky to give a delicate, ethereal illumination to the scene in the opposite direction. Delicate is in any case the keyword here. Good twilight is soft and unpredictable,

and the changes in color and intensity tend to happen a lot faster than you notice.

There is also an important difference in the way that you see a scene as it moves into twilight. The retina has two different systems — photopic vision for bright light, with full color response, and scotopic vision for low light, with more sensitivity to light but poorer color distinction and resolution. The changeover from one to the other takes time. At the end of the day, the scene is getting darker, and the eye and brain take longer to adapt than in the opposite situation, when the scene is getting lighter. This is partly due to familiarity, as fewer people experience daybreak than sunset, but the usual impression as night turns into day is that things are brighter than they really are. If you begin shooting so early in the morning that there is no light in the sky, just before sunrise everything will appear completely bright. Practically, it is important to keep checking the results on the camera's LCD screen, as your own visual judgment, particularly of color, may not be as reliable as you think. An important caveat here, as already mentioned

earlier, is that at this time of day the preview image on the screen can be misleading in brightness. It, of course, stays at a constant brightness while the scene around it is either fading or brightening, so it is very common to underexpose if you go by the screen image alone. At twilight, the screen's backlighting is much brighter than that of the surroundings, and this exaggerates the brightness of the image as shot, so always check the histogram as well.

Other than pure, natural landscapes, twilight also brings artificial lighting into play. After sunset, street

Dusk wedding
Captured at f2.8, this dusk scene looks well lit though the chromiance noise is something of a give away.

lighting is switched on, as are interior lights in houses and offices, flood-lighting and display lighting. These may or may not be what you expect or want, and will often affect the composition. Lighting in cities tends to be different at each end of the day throughout the year. If you want the maximum amount of interior lighting visible in office blocks, for example, the best time is usually just after sunset in winter, when most people are still working.

True night photography is when there is not even a trace of residual light from the sun, and this offers a few, limited possibilities (discounting astrophotography, which is a specialization too specific to deal with here). Mainly, night photography is practical when there is a clear moon and the phase is somewhere between half and full. This was both difficult and uncertain in the days of film, but digital technology has now opened this up to non-specialists.

The moon, of course, reflects sunlight, so for lighting purposes a full moon behaves like a very dim sun. A figure often quoted, and useful, is 250,000 times dimmer, which is 18 stops as a camera setting. Thus, to revive the "sunny 16" rule mentioned previously, the exposure for a high, full, unclouded moon would be 18 stops less than 1/100 sec at $f16$ and ISO 100. This gives about 1 minute at $f2.8$. This is a reasonable starting point for an "average" full moon exposure, meaning within a day or two of perfectly full (0° phase angle), within 15° of directly overhead, and in clear air. Unlike film, sensors do not suffer from reciprocity failure, so this exposure needs no further adjustment.

In practice it is very difficult to judge the brightness of moonlight because it varies so much. There are several factors that affect this, and the phase is the

Moonlight
The Moon is 250,000 times dimmer than the sun, but is reflecting the same light.

City Lights
Pudong at night, seen across the Huangpu River from the Bund, Shanghia, China.

Moonlight and artificial light create contrasting colors in this image.

most important. Between full and a quarter the brightness varies by an order of magnitude — about 3½ stops. The orbits of the earth around the sun and the moon around the earth also vary, so the sun distance changes by 7% and the moon distance by 30%, which combines to make a difference of about a third of a stop. The opposition effect, in which there is a sudden increase of brightness when the moon is almost exactly opposite the sun, caused by the high reflectivity of the moon's surface, adds another third of a stop of variance. Finally, atmospheric attenuation because of moisture, dust, and the height of the moon above the horizon can make a difference of up to 8 *f* stops (over 2 orders of magnitude).

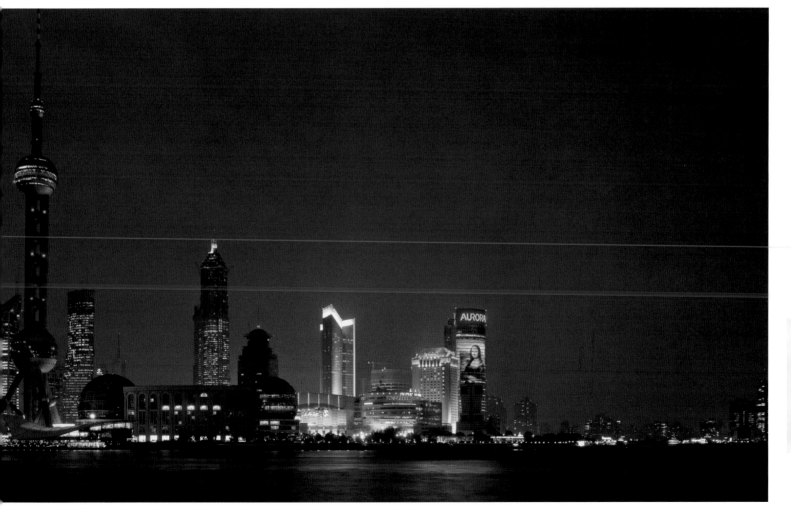

ARTIFICIAL LOW LIGHT

Lamps that work by burning filaments are the most traditional kind of artificial illumination, with a low color temperature but a continuous spectrum. Specifically, the color temperature of a light source depends on the energy output (in watts), as we saw on pages 18-19, and is significantly orange in relation to daylight. Because incandescent lamps and the sun generate light by the same mechanism — burning — they are perfectly known quantities and are no problem for photography.

Artificial lighting is moving gradually from incandescent to non-incandescent, because of cost-efficiency and global energy concerns. In general, this is bad news for photography, but digital techniques can help.

Non-incandescent lighting, however, is another matter, and is increasing in use. Most modern artificial lighting relies on the visible emissions from specific elements, which are always limited and never as pleasing as continuous-spectrum light. The development of lighting engineering has led to a growing variety of these non-incandescent lamps (another description often used is non-black-body lighting). All of them, from fluorescent to vapor discharge lights, make use of specific chemical elements

Tungsten halogen
Downlighters used here in a modern Japanese tea ceremony room are low-voltage (12v) tungsten halogen lamps. These burn brighter and hotter than standard incandescent lamps, and so at a slightly higher color temperature, and the low-voltage variety can be made smaller.

TUNGSTEN VS FLUORESCENT

The problem for interior photography, as shown in the main sequence of images here, becomes entirely understandable when the spectral power distribution is compared between tungsten (left) and fluorescent (at 5000 K, right). Not only is the red deficient, but more important, there are green spikes from the mercury.

2800 K Incandescent house lamp

5000 K Flourescent
Notice the mercury energy spikes

Display window
Incandescent lamps behind a diffused screen at a restaurant. The diffusion spreads the fall-off in illumination around each lamp, and also the apparent color. Over-exposure near the center of each lamp records as close to white, shading to yellow and orange as it becomes darker.

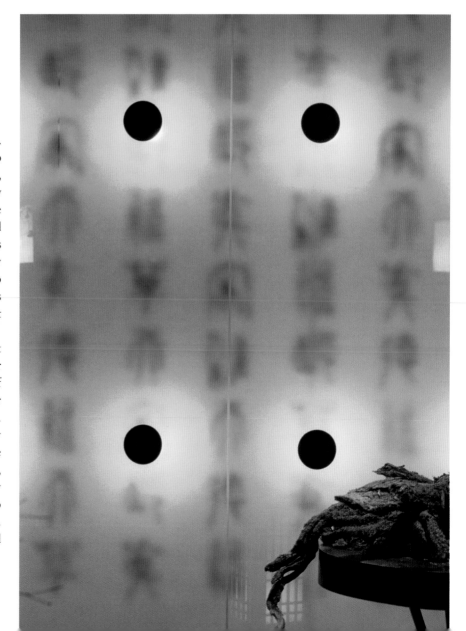

that are in one way or another excited to emit light. However, while incandescent light — from the sun to a flame — emits a continuous spectrum of wavelengths, individual chemical elements emit just a very narrow part of the spectrum. The emission spectra for these lamps have the appearance of a group of isolated narrow spikes. No single element on its own gives anything like the full spectrum of daylight, but by carefully choosing a group of elements it is possible to get close to its appearance to the human eye. This is mimicking a continuous light source, and how well it does this depends on the engineering design.

What matters to photographers is artificial light that is close to the quality of either sunlight or incandescent lamps, but this is only one of the aims of lighting designers. Other things may have a higher priority, such as efficiency, brightness, and cost. Ultimately, judgments about lighting are largely subjective, but in the lighting industry there are attempts to quantify it. One key concept is chromaticity, which is a measure of the quality of light as defined by its purity and dominant wavelength. Purity is akin to saturation and the wavelength is equivalent to hue. Both the CCT (Correlated Color Temperature) and the CIE x and y coordinates define this.

ARTIFICIAL LOW LIGHT

But because lighting that does not have a continuous spectrum is unlikely to be perfect in the way it renders all colors of all objects, another scale is needed, one that rates the lighting based on visual experience. The Color Rendering Index (CRI) is used by manufacturers to give an idea of how closely their products come to continuous lighting as perceived by viewers. It is based on a viewing test of eight pastel color swatches, which admittedly is not very many, and is one measure of metamerism (see the box on page 55). Both daylight and artificial incandescent light rate 100 on a scale from 0 to 100. The very best fluorescent lamps reach about 90, but poorer, cheaper ones can rate as low as

Fluorescent in context
A compromise white balance for an evening shot that includes fluorescent lighting on the ground floor of this modern Japanese house, tungsten on the floors above, and a clear sky behind, reveals the essential greenness of typical fluorescent lighting.

QUALITY OF LIGHT

Light source	CRI
Sunlight	100
100W incandescent lamp	100
metal halide 5400 K	93
deluxe pro warm white (Philips)	92
deluxe cool white fluorescent	86
metal halide 4200 K	83
daylight fluorescent	76
deluxe warm white fluorescent	73
cool white fluorescent	65
warm white fluorescent	55
white deluxe mercury	45
high pressure sodium	25
clear mercury	17
low pressure sodium	0-18

Source: Illuminating Engineering Society. Interim Method of Measuring and Specifying Color Rendering of Light Sources, LM-19, NY, 1962.

50, while some vapor discharge lamps, such as sodium, can be much lower still. Another view of the CRI is that it is a measure of how "pleasing" a light source is, and indeed this ultimately is what is important in most photography. All the settings and post-production work that goes into correcting images shot under fluorescent and vapor discharge lighting is essentially concerned with making the results believable and pleasing. Fluorescent and the various flavors of vapor discharge lamps differ considerably in the way they work, but for photography they present essentially the same (and considerable) problems.

FLUORESCENT LIGHT

Fluorescent lighting is spreading, particularly in homes and other spaces that were traditionally lit with tungsten. Concerns about energy conservation are encouraging this kind of conversion, and while photographically fluorescents are less predictable than incandescent, this is an inevitable process of change. Clearly, the ability to set the white balance in a digital camera makes all this manageable in a way that it was not with traditional film, but there are still issues.

Fluorescent lamps work by passing an electric current through a gas-filled glass envelope, typically a long circular tube (hence the popular name strip-lighting). The gas produces ultraviolet light that strikes the coating on the inside of the tube, which is a coating composed of a mixture of fluorescent compounds. These fluoresce (glow), for as long as they are bombarded with the ultraviolet light. The newest types have coiled tubes to make them suitable for replacing standard tungsten fixtures, and are known as CFL (Compact Fluorescent Lamps).

Because each of the fluorescers emits light in a very narrow band of the visible spectrum, the skill in designing these lamps lies in blending a range of them so as to approximate the full continuous spectrum that we are accustomed to from white or incandescent light. The key word, nevertheless, is "approximate," because there are always spikes, or gaps, or both in the emission spectra of fluorescent lamps. The human eye accommodates well to this slightly broken spectrum, and of course most of them are designed for human vision. The camera sensor, however, reveals any imperfections all too clearly. Fluorescent lamp design varies widely, not only on the scale of cool to warm (lamps tend to be classified as cool-white, warm-white

and so on), but in the color casts they give that are not visible to the eye at the time. Even the high CRI scores given by manufacturers do not tell the entire story. The spectral energy distribution is not coherent and there will always be some discrepancies in yellow and green, as well as poor coverage in red and blue.

The important thing to remember is that in most photographs it is the appearance that counts. Occasionally, you may have a need for absolute accuracy, and there are ways of doing this (see the section "Profiling for color" on pages 64-65), but most of the time the color simply needs to look acceptable to someone viewing the finished image. The white balance camera settings are the first point of

Subway
A new Tokyo subway station uses fluorescent lighting as part of the design. With the view consisting of simple concrete walls and ceiling, Auto white balance is an easy and satisfactory solution.

ARTIFICIAL LOW LIGHT

DOMESTIC FLUORESCENT FITTINGS

The strips above the work surfaces are typical of many modern kitchens, and the problem is the skewed spectrum with emission spikes in yellow-green, making a perfect color balance impossible. Corrective actions tend towards a monochrome appearance.

A range of three different exposures shows that the problem is not confined to an overall color cast, but to color shifts with brightness. The work surface should be white, and the kettle and metal fittings gray.

Because the image as shot includes other lighting (daylight and tungsten), the best compromise for all resulted in this greenish cast for the kitchen areas, evident in this section viewed in Photoshop's raw converter.

Basic	
White Balance:	Fluorescent
Temperature	3800
Tint	+21
	Auto Default
Exposure	0.00
Recovery	0
Fill Light	0
Blacks	5
Brightness	+50
Contrast	+25
	☐ Convert to Grayscale
Vibrance	0
Saturation	0

The preset fluorescent balance is only a slight improvement.

Using the white balance dropper on the back wall gives a general neutrality, but also loss of color saturation and, in the context of the entire shot, too cool an appearance.

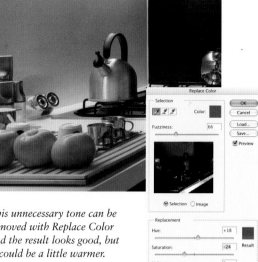

Lowering the color temperature gives a warmer, more natural appearance, but the general effect is still too monochromatic.

As most of the color resides in the reds, one solution is to increase red and orange saturation. This is an improvement, but it turns the front edge of the work surface red at the same time.

This unnecessary tone can be removed with Replace Color and the result looks good, but it could be a little warmer.

An orange filter gives an overall warmth to this section of the image, and enhances the color of the apples.

ARTIFICIAL LOW LIGHT

control, essential if you are shooting JPEG or TIFF, less so if you are shooting Raw. The difference is that with the first two formats, the camera will process the image and deliver a particular color balance as you shoot. With Raw, the white balance settings are kept separately from the Raw capture data, allowing you to choose which color temperature and hue/tint you prefer during post-production.

Clearly, as long as you don't mind spending extra time on the computer, Raw has the advantage. Nevertheless, even though any white balance can be chosen at this later stage, there are some advantages to choosing the best-looking white balance at the time of shooting. One is that it gives you an opportunity to check the result at the time by comparing the LCD screen with the scene. Admittedly, the camera screen does not give an ideally calibrated view, but it is better than nothing. The fluorescent settings (there may be more than one according to the model of camera) are the obvious choice, but as fluorescent color casts are unpredictable, they are not necessarily the best. Also consider trying the auto setting, and varying the color adjustment if your camera has this. With more time available, consider setting a custom white balance, although this can be a complicated procedure.

In any case, you must judge the way the color of the scene looks to you in some way, and this is especially important for Raw shooting. It often helps to remember a key color, and if there is a gray or other shade of neutral in the scene, this is worth noting. If you have time, one great help is to place a color target such as the Gretag Macbeth ColorChecker, in the

Outdoor vapor discharge
The foreground lighting in this night-time view of the Golden Temple, Amritsar, is vapor discharge. This strongly blue-green light, contrasts with the orange of the incandescent-lit Golden Temple itself, behind. In this instance, the color contrast helps the image.

Bloomberg display
A display booth for the financial information service provider Bloomberg is lit from below with vapor discharge lamps. In this case, the unusual atmosphere of the room is better handled by allowing it to stay blue. Full correction would have less visual impact.

DIFFERENT LIGHTS, DIFFERENT COLORS

The problem of the sometimes strange cast from a broken spectrum can go beyond just the sensor's reaction. The eye also can receive different color information from that seen under daylight. Metamerism is when two color surfaces appear the same under one light (such as daylight) but different from each other under another light (as often happens with fluorescent lighting). This doubles the difficulty of judging how a scene should appear, and there is no obvious solution. Just be aware that some colors may shift independently of the majority.

Flourescent lighting
This underground railway station platform is lit with Flourescent lighting. In the far distance, it is apparent a different kind of lighting is used in the stairway.

River Ganges
The celebration of music and prayer on the banks of the Ganges at Rishikesh, Uttarkand, India, takes place at sunrise and sunset.

Artist's studio
A Beijing artist's studio lit by multi-vapor lamps high in the ceiling. In this kind of situation, in which there is no other lighting for comparison, and in which the colors of the paintings need to be accurate (that is, grays neutral), aiming for a neutral white balance is the best option.

ARTIFICIAL LOW LIGHT

scene and take a reference shot. Unless you need total accuracy, you do not need to perform a thorough profiling—simply being able to compare the target visually with the image is likely to be sufficient. You can also perform a basic balance by using the Gray Point dropper in Curves or Levels.

VAPOR DISCHARGE LIGHT

Now more widely used, vapor discharge lamps are capable of high output and come in several flavors, the color depending largely on the type of gas. They share their basic principle with fluorescent lamps passing an electrical discharge through a gas. Here the gas contains metal vapor, which emits light, and Mercury is one of the principal components. The problem for photography is in the broken spectrum and emission spikes, and also in the shortage of long red wavelengths. The eye is less sensitive to the missing long red wavelengths than both film and sensors, and tends to accommodate the color output, seeing it as more or less white, while the sensor records it as more blue-green. In addition, red surfaces in a scene will tend to look darker and duller, again because of the deficiency in longer red wavelengths.

Mixed lighting: welding
The temperature at the tip of a welding arc typically exceeds 6500 K, giving a bluish light when seen against thebackground filtered daylight in this studio.

Mixed lighting: market
A street market in Kuala Lumpur contains a mix of daylight with 2800 K incandescent lamps hanging over each stall.

Mixed lighting: daylight and incandescent
Daylight reflected from a courtyard entering the scene from the right, contrasts with the incandescent lighting entering (behind the blue sign) from the left. Their effect is very noticeable on the white clothing of this priest in a Shanghai temple. As in many other situations, two opposed lighting sources in one image has the potential to be attractive rather than be a problem.

FIREWORKS

A few subjects reveal themselves in an image only by means of motion blur. One of the most obvious is a firework display. Even to the human eye, it is the rapid movement of points of light appearing as streaks that create the intended effect. A sharply frozen image taken at a short shutter speed would look like nothing more than bright points. Unless there is a significant amount of drifting smoke illuminated by the explosions, the shutter speed will have no significant effect on the overall brightness of the scene; instead, it determines the length of the streak in the frame. Generally, the longer the better, although it is usually sensible to keep one exposure to one burst of the display. The wider the angle of lens, the more certain you are of framing the display fully, but in any case, pay attention to the first burst for predicting the position of subsequent bursts in the sky. An alternative technique with a telephoto lens is to loosen the tripod head slightly, follow the rocket trail upwards, and when it reaches its highest point, quickly lock the head and open the shutter.

COLOR TEMPERATURE BLENDING

One fairly obvious method of handling a scene lit by different types of light source with opposing color balances is to treat it as two (or more) layers, one for each light source. The principle is to concentrate first on color correction for each light source, layer at a time, and save the problem of combining them until later. Thus, for one image layer, you should focus entirely on only for one light source, ignoring the effects this has on parts lit by any other source. For the next layer, do the same for the other light source. With three or more different light sources this can become unnecessarily complicated, but with two it is perfectly manageable.

In a classic two-light-source setting, consider making two image versions, each with a different white balance, and using layers to combine them.

The color adjustment method can be any of the ones discussed previously, including setting the Gray Point or White Point, applying a complementary overall color filter (Photo Filter in Photoshop), Hue/Saturation sliders, Color Balance sliders, and others. This depends very much on being able to identify which parts of the scene have been lit — and therefore color-shifted — by which light source, and this will be easier in some photographs than in others.

The next step is to blend the two (or more) layers in a sensible and realistic way. Again, Photoshop offers a huge variety of ways of doing this, but it is probably wise not to get obsessed with the relative merits of each method. In the end, we are dealing pragmatically with photographs. If the influence of each light source is clearly related to an obvious value, such as brightness, there is likely to be a procedure that can blend the layers simply. In the example here of the Japanese table detail, the brightness of the recessed

BLENDING OPTIONS

A glass artwork set in a table and lit from beneath. Photographing it at dusk gives a choice of two very different color temperatures. Fortunately, most of the incandescent lighting is at the high end of the tonal range, giving the opportunity to blend the two images as layers, selecting the blend on the basis of brightness (more orange version underneath)

Incandescent white balance

Daylight white balance

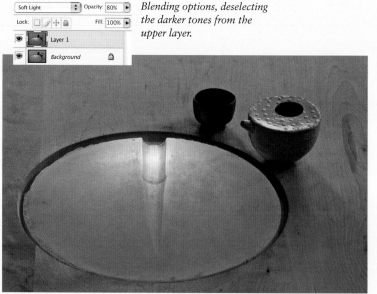

Blending options, deselecting the darker tones from the upper layer.

The final result

MANUAL ERASE

A different approach to the same problem. Daylight entering from the small window contrasts sharply and not very pleasantly with the incandescent lighting of this bathroom.

Incandescent white balance

Daylight white balance

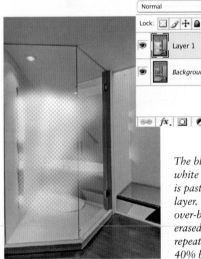

The bluer (incandescent white balance) version is pasted in as the upper layer. The unwanted, over-blue areas are erased manually with repeated strokes of a 40% brush.

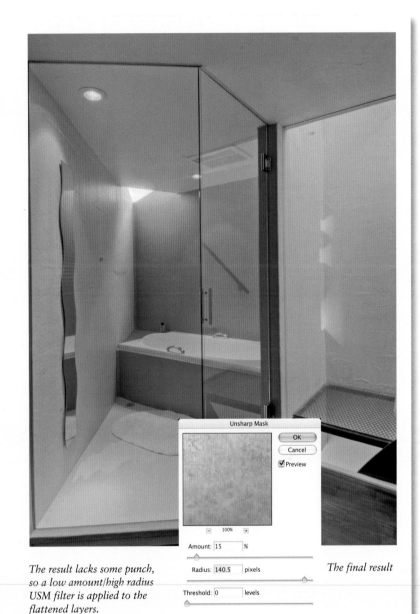

The result lacks some punch, so a low amount/high radius USM filter is applied to the flattened layers.

The final result

glass lamp meant that incandescent lighting, at around 3000 K, affected most of the highlights in the scene, while the shadow areas were for the most part lit by the much bluer evening daylight (around 6000 K). This made a procedural blend an easy choice, using some trial and error with the Blending Options from the Layers palette, and settling on Soft Light.

Otherwise, a hands-on approach using erasing or brushing, allows more personal choices. One obvious choice is to erase the "wrongly lit" areas from the upper layer, paying careful attention to the size,

opacity percentage, and hardness of the brush. Another is to use the History Brush. In this case, one method is to make the necessary color adjustments to one image, add another layer with its own, different adjustments, flatten the image, and use the History Brush tool to restore selectively from the original. This is more complicated to set up, but some people find restoring more intuitive than erasing. If you are using brushes in any of these ways, make sure that the number of History States is set high enough in Preferences before you start.

SELECTIVE COLOR CHANGE

A direct approach to the problem of mixed light sources is to select the color effect of one and then shift it or filter it towards a more pleasing or neutral result. There are a number of ways of targeting specific colors in an image, and these vary according to the image-editing software. Beginning with Photoshop, the two most convenient are Replace Color (see box, page 63) and Hue/Saturation, both found under *Image>Adjustments*. Hue/Saturation has been around for a long time, and Replace Color is actually a more focused version of the procedure, with an accompanying preview of the areas selected. In either case, the technique involves first selecting the most intense area of the offending color, adjusting the range of the selection (called Fuzziness in the case of Replace Color, while shown as arrows on a color bar in Hue/Saturation). The three parameter sliders Hue, Saturation, and Lightness can then be adjusted to taste. In Hue/Saturation, once you have selected a color range from the drop-down menu, clicking on part of the image will refine that selection. A third procedure that is less intuitive, is Selective Color, also under *Image>Adjustments*.

There are two possible drawbacks to these otherwise excellent and easy techniques. One is that the choice of color alteration is not fully flexible. It relies on Hue shift by degree, Saturation, and Lightness, and misses out on arbitrary color filtering (such as Photo Filter, also under *Image>Adjustments*) and contrast control. The other drawback is when a targeted color also covers other objects and surfaces in an image that you do not want to change. In the latter case, for example, imagine a blue vase in an interior view lit by both incandescent and daylight. If you decide to select the blue cast from daylight and shift that, the same effect will happen to the vase. A sensible and manageable solution is to use the History brush to restore those areas.

A more laborious, but potentially more accurate, method of selection is to define the areas of the image that you want to change. There are several ways of doing this, including such selection tools as the Magic Wand, Quick Selection tool, or Color range feature to name a few. These create selections that can then be modified by expanding, contracting, selecting similar values, and so on. Alternatively, there is direct mask painting, which can then be used as a selection. Often, selection is more accurate by using a combination of these methods, for instance a quick selection by first using the Magic Wand, converting this into a mask, then modifying by erasing and painting, and possibly blurring.

Other image-editing programs offer different solutions. In DxO Optics Pro, the Multi-Point Color Balance tool negates the need for selection by allowing the user to shift several points while viewing a preview on the right of the screen (see box, right).

LightZone, a relatively new entrant in the image-editing software market, is interesting because it is aimed fully at photographers and tries to keep the language and metaphors for working on digital images simple and familiar. Of particular interest in area selection is the introduction of regions (see box, page 62). This is a concept that is designed to make it possible to make detailed local changes in what would otherwise be a global image-editing program (similar to Adobe Lightroom or Apple Aperture). This makes non-destructive editing much more easily accessible to photographers who have become used to the many tools in "traditional" image editors (like Adobe Photoshop) which act on specific areas of an image.

> **Possibly the most controlled technique for adjusting a variety of color shifts in a single image is to use hue-specific selection and adjustment in post-production.**

DXO

Color balancing in DxO Optics Pro, called Multi-Point Color balance, allows several points to be clicked, and then the color shift specified by dragging around a color wheel.

The image as opened in DxO, original on the left, changes applied on the right. This is the default, with some automatic corrections.

The third and final sample is on the stalactites at right, which are too "hot" because of incandescent lighting.

The first point is in the shaft of light, which I want to be neutral. Note that sampling very bright tones can create huge shifts in the rest of the range, but this will be taken care of in the next sample.

The second sample is in the water, which I want to make more vivid. The sample shifts are recorded in the small squares at lower right.

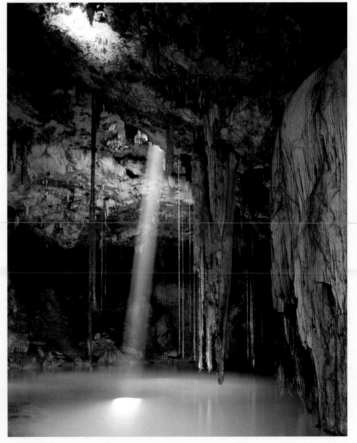

Result

SELECTIVE COLOR CHANGE

LIGHTZONE

In LightZone, we make use here of one of its most powerful features; a fast, intuitive area selection.

Compared with the daylight illuminating the near ceiling tiles, the furthest part of the room appears too "hot."

With White Balance selected, a bezier curve is drawn around the area to be changed.

The gap between the outer and inner boundaries is the transition zone. Selecting the inner boundary, this is then dragged inwards to enlarge the zone for a smoother final effect.

The color temperature slider is dragged slightly to the left.

The final result

PHOTOSHOP REPLACE COLOR

We can make use of Photoshop's Replace Color tool to replace areas of color without selecting them separately.

The exact sample points are critical. Red dots mark the points sampled, and show the importance of finding the point that encompasses the entire area that we want to shift.

With the precise sampling point finalized, the hue is lowered slightly, as is the saturation, and the lightness increased, all to match the rest of the steps.

Original

Using Selective Color, the yellows are chosen, and their precise hue manipulated for a more neutral, creamier effect.

The result, almost perfect, although judged a little too yellow.

The final result

PROFILING FOR COLOR

As we've seen, even though many interiors are lit by a variety of light sources of uncertain color temperature and quality, corrections of many kinds can be made in post-production. For most photography, the overall appearance is all that counts—if it looks fine, it is fine—but when absolute color fidelity is important (textiles, fashion, logos, and so on), we need an objective standard. This is where color targets come in, and the one of choice is inevitably the renown Gretag Macbeth ColorChecker.

One way of achieving greater color accuracy is to shoot a standard color target in the same lighting, then use this to create a camera profile.

The procedure is to shoot this target under exactly the same lighting conditions as the photograph. Having done this, you can later make a profile for this combination of camera and light that you can apply to the pictures taken at the same time. This, at least, is the theory, although there will still be discrepancies if the interior space you are photographing is lit differently in different parts. It's also important to remember that the results are good for only this one time, and the particular camera and sensor.

In practice, place the target so that it is evenly lit, full-face to the camera, and almost filling the frame. Reset all hue adjustments in the camera, and choose a standard, appropriate, white balance. Expose for an average rendering, and remember that the black patch is dark gray, very far from black. Avoid highlight clipping. The ideal exposure should be about 10 levels down from maximum for the white patch (around 245) and around 50 levels up from maximum for the black (around 50).

The next step is to create the profile. The software used here is inCamera from Pictographics. This is a Photoshop plug-in. Make sure that all warnings are turned on in Photoshop's Color Settings (not in the preferences, as you might expect, but an option called "Check when opening" found in the *Edit > Color Settings* dialog). When you open the image containing the color target, if the warning "Embedded Profile Mismatch" appears, choose "Discard the embedded profile." If the warning "Missing Profile" appears, choose "Leave as is." Adjust the lightness of the image with Levels or Curves to achieve the following values for white (RGB 243 or, if there is a strong color cast, Lightness 96 in Lab mode) and for black RGB 52 or Lightness 20. Launch the profiling software, align the grid to compensate for any perspective distortion as shown, select the ColorChecker target that you used (the ColorChecker is not the only color target on the market, though it might be the most famous), and finally name and save the profile created. When you open the real image file that you shot at the same time as the target, you can access this new profile through *Edit > Assign Profile*. Last of all, choose "Convert to Profile" to convert it to your normal working color space (the most widely used is the Adobe RGB (1998) space).

THE MAKING OF A COLOR TARGET

The reason for the universal acceptance of the GretagMacbeth ColorCheker, and its high cost, is that it's color swatches are made to extremely high standards, and individually checked at the manufacturer's. The basic target of 24 patches is a measured and known quantity. The values are published for chromaticity, luminosity, and Munsell hue, value, and chroma. The RGB values are less accurate and less useful. Profiling software makes use of these known values by comparing them with the actual capture. From the difference, a cross-spectrum correction can be calculated, then applied to any image shot under the same light.

Before

A shot of the target propped in front of the scene to be photographed, is opened in Photoshop's raw converter. Exposure is adjusted slightly so that the white and black patches are well within range (ideally 243 for white and 52 for black). There is no other adjustment, certainly not for the color.

Before

The more advanced digital ColorChecker is used here. The lighting in this banqueting hall is fluorescent and quite unpleasant.

Chart Type:
ColorChecker®DC

(Data Reference File...)
ColorChecker DC.txt

☐ Show Samples
☐ Ignore Glossy
☐ Brighter
☐ Use Largest Window

Profile Name for Display:
18625files

Profiling tool 1

Using the inCamera plug-in from PictoColor, the image is opened, the target type selected, and a name given for the profile (the name of the file in this case).

Profiling tool 2

The grid is adjusted to fit by dragging the corner points.

The profile is saved

Test

To check for accuracy, the same image of the target is opened and saved in Photoshop with the identical settings, then the saved profile is assigned to it. The result is perfect across the range.

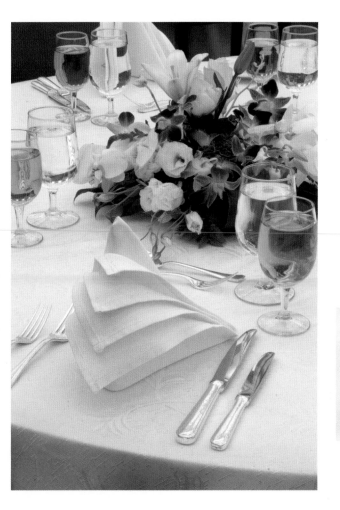

Result

The final image with new color profile.

SECTION 2 **HAND HELD**

As I mentioned at the beginning of this book, one of the outstanding practical features of lowlight photography is that you are always pushing the limits. And these are, first and foremost, technical limits, with a clear, smoothly-toned image being the reference standard. The goal is almost always is to reach the best possible balance between sharpness and noise. Sharpness, as we're about to see in this chapter, is a huge area of importance and covers much more than most people might imagine. This is why I plan to devote many pages to it, because in lowlight photography more than most kinds, an essential skill is to be able to judge sharpness and unsharpness to a particularly fine degree.

In practice, setting out for a lowlight shoot requires a key decision—whether or not to use a tripod. On the face of it this may sound a little trivial, but it has far-reaching consequences. The two paths, hand held or tripod shooting, are each suited to different subjects and conditions, and they are widely divergent in style. They also depend on a decision before planning the photography, because unless you are fortunate enough to have an assistant or a willing companion to carry things, what you set out with in your camera bag and on your shoulder will determine the kind of photography you can do.

In this chapter, I want to look at the tripod-free approach, relying on hand-holding skills to get as close to normal, rapid-reaction, reportage photography as possible. Here, your own physical skills become important, especially how steadily and reliably you can hold and operate the camera. Professionals take some pride in doing this, but they are by no means immune to failure, precisely because they are pushing limits. One thing that lowlight photographers quickly get used to when shooting without rock-steady support is there is always a failure rate. Of x number of frames shot, y will be flawed because of blur of one kind or another. The aim is to bring the number y down as much as possible, and reduce the proportion of failures. Indeed, if every frame were technically perfect, this would be a sign that you were not pushing the limits as hard as you could.

HAND HELD OR LOCKED DOWN

Lowlight photography divides into two very different ways of working, influenced mainly by the subject matter, but also the technical image quality that you need.

Lowlight photography is one area in which process dominates. By this I mean that all the various limits and difficulties that we looked at in the first chapter need to be thought about before you start shooting. In practical terms, lowlight shooting is about pushing technical and mechanical limits as far as you can, and this in turn means that there are two competing ways of approaching it. In one—the subject of this chapter—the idea is to do everything necessary to retain the freedom of using a camera in much the same way as you would under normal light. The alternative is to abandon freedom in favor of a full choice of technical settings—sharp, clean images without noise, and at any aperture setting, and with no limit to the exposure time (except, of course, for short exposures).

It is not easy to switch from one to the other mid-shoot, so it is normal to decide at the start which route you are going to take for any one session. There are good arguments for both hand-held and for using a tripod, and which to choose depends on the subject, your preferred style, the results you are looking for and the quality you absolutely need. The last factor is too often ignored, as we'll come to in a moment, and can sometimes make the others redundant.

The key factor for most photographers is the optimum shutter speed for subject movement. If the subject is active, instance people in motion, a tripod is no help in freezing the movement. Some kinds of movement may well be acceptable, or even desirable, such as the streaked trails of vehicle lights on a highway, but if you need sharp capture, the threshold shutter speed for this determines everything. This in turn is affected by the relative movement in the image frame (see pages 124-127), so a walking figure naturally calls for a faster shutter speed if it fills the frame than if it takes up just a small part of the picture. But basically, the rule is if you are photographing people, then shoot hand held.

The obvious advantages are freedom and mobility, and the chance to shoot unobserved, without drawing attention to the camera as is inevitable with a tripod. You can strip down the amount of equipment drastically; one camera, one or two lenses, maybe a flash unit if the camera does not have one built in, and very little else. Gone are the days of two camera bodies, each for a different film (such as high-speed color, with high-speed black and white to be pushed to the maximum if necessary). Digitally, everything can be dialled up from the menu.

Subject motion sets limits
Hand held shooting reaches its practical limit when the movement of subjects is too fast even for a combination of wide-open aperture and high ISO setting. This is a tripod shot at 1/10 sec, making deliberate use of the blur of a passerby.

HAND HELD

Lowlight reportage
Shooting hand held means being able to follow classic reportage methods, which include quick observation and photographing unnoticed. The difference is the lower light levels. Here, at a museum in Shanghai, bracing against a wall allowed a shutter speed of 1/4 sec with a 33 mm efl, and a low ISO setting of 100.

Size matters
While noise is evident at 100% magnification on the computer screen, in print and at this size of reproduction, it becomes unnoticeable. Size of use is always an important consideration.

Shooting light
The choice to shoot hand held makes it possible, with digital camera technology, to strip down the equipment to bare essentials: here a single camera body with two lenses, one a wide-ratio zoom with vibration-reduction system, the other a fast, fixed focal length lens for specific situations where subject movement needs to be caught.

Detail
Remember to use the 100% magnification to check pixel-level detail.

HAND HELD OR LOCKED DOWN

The disadvantages are in camera handling and image quality. As hand held shooting in these conditions almost never enjoys the luxury of fast shutter speeds, holding the camera (and yourself) still is always an issue, and may often — as we'll see a few pages further on — call for over-shooting to lessen the risk of frames lost to camera shake. A fast lens, with a maximum aperture wider then $f2$, is a distinct advantage, though costly. Image quality centers on noise, because the key strategy is setting the appropriate ISO. High sensitivity means high noise levels, and while there are ways of dealing with this it reduces quality. This completely depends on how the pictures are going to be used, in particular the size. It is very important to become familiar with just how bad different noise levels look when reproduced at particular scales. The positive side of this is that if you are going to use the picture small, the noise may be invisible, thus giving hand held almost no disadvantages at all.

HAND HELD v LOCKED DOWN

Hand held	Locked down
Free, quick, and mobile	Static, takes time to change viewpoint
Unobtrusive, allows reportage-style shooting	Conspicuous, may attract unwanted attention
Lightweight, needs little equipment	Tripod can be an inconvenient burden
First choice for subjects in motion	First choice for static subjects
Camera shake always an issue	If tripod used well, no risk of camera shake
Fast lenses are a priority	Any lens can be used, even very long slow telephotos
Needs high ISO settings, resulting in noise	Can use lowest ISO setting
Depth of field always shallow because wide apertures used	Good depth of field practical by stopping down

Hand held movement
Hand held shooting allows for a number of loose, ad hoc effects, such as a slow speed while walking, as in this image, taken at 1/3 sec.

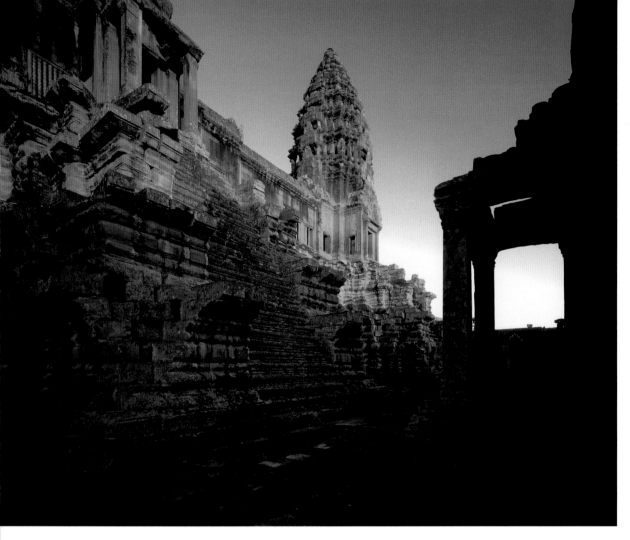

Depth of detail
Images that rely heavily on fine resolution of detail, and which are likely to be used large, such as this formal architectural view of Angkor Wat, call for maximum image quality. Noise artifacts are especially unwelcome, so a tripod is the natural choice.

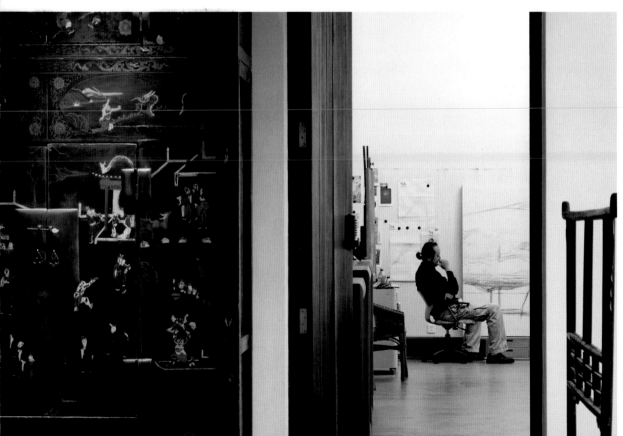

Depth of field
When full depth of field is called for, in order to juxtapose near and far subjects and keep them sharp, the shutter speed is likely to be too low for a hand held shot. In this portrait of a Chinese artist, Shao Fan, the EFL on the zoom was 100 mm. An aperture of f16 in available light at ISO 100, and therefore a shutter speed of 3 sec, made a tripod a necessity.

STEADYING TECHNIQUES

Slow shutter speeds are inevitable in low light, and there are a number of ways of improving your threshold for avoiding camera shake.

The ability to hold a camera steady tends to be assumed, and the general opinion is that you either can or cannot. In fact, it can always be improved by following certain techniques and by training yourself in specific ways. In normal lighting and with standard camera settings, this is rarely an issue, as shutter speeds of at least 1/125 sec are usually possible. When the shutter speed needs to be longer, as in 1/30 sec, 1/15 sec and slower, camera shake becomes a pressing problem. At worst, you lose shots, while at best you waste time checking the image after each shot to confirm that it is sharp. Lowlight photography, with its typically slow shutter speeds, is when you most need to be able to hold a camera steadily enough to remain on the subject.

On pages 96 to 103 we'll look in detail at what happens to the image under the influence of camera shake, but the issue is whether the image moves sufficiently in the time allowed for the exposure to be noticeable. This boils down to the speed of the twitch or jitter, which determines what distance the image jerks across the frame. An important secondary factor is the focal length of the lens. A longer focal length magnifies the image more, and this magnifies any movements, including camera shake. A widely accepted standard is that camera shake is unlikely at a shutter speed that is the reciprocal of the focal length, because most people can hold steady at such a speed. Thus 1/100 sec with a 100 mm lens should carry no risk.

These are reasonable and slightly conservative estimates, but any serious photographer should aim to improve on them, provided you do not suffer from any condition which makes it impossible. When seeking that improvement, it makes sense to turn to activities that rely totally on holding a piece of equipment steady against a distant object. There is much to learn from rifle shooting and from archery, where there is a rich history of training and practice in aiming and hitting targets. In photography, locking on to the "target" is only one step in the complex process of making an image, but in low light it becomes especially important.

The first step is to know what you are capable of, and the way to do this, as well as to improve and train, is a kind of target practice. Photographing meaningless subjects may be anathema to many people, but frankly it is better to test your hand-holding abilities when the results do not matter. As always, it is best to avoid on-the-job training. Take a stationary subject that is convenient, at an easy focusable distance, and which has good sharp detail. Printed type is good, as in an optician's. Make this a test that is practical for your own way of shooting, so assemble the lenses you normally use. If a zoom, decide on certain focal lengths, such as both ends of the scale and two or three points between, depending on the zoom range. Set the camera to shutter priority. Take a series of identically framed shots at one focal length. Begin a shutter speed high enough to guarantee sharpness — for instance, twice that of the reciprocal of the focal length, as 1/200 sec with a 100 mm lens. This will be the reference. Then set the shutter speed to half as fast and take three shots. Adjust the shutter speed to half as fast again and take three more shots. Follow the steps shown in the table (see page 74). The reason for shooting three frames for each setting is that camera shake is unpredictable.

MOVEMENT AND FOCAL LENGTH

The amount of movement revealed by camera shake depends on the magnification, and so is proportionate to the focal length. These are the relative movements of the same amount of shake at three different focal lengths. Wide-angle shots suffer the least of all.

50mm

100mm

200mm

Extremely sharp

Acceptably sharp

Slight motion blur

Significant motion blur

Extreme motion blur

STEADYING TECHNIQUES

TESTING YOURSELF

Examine the results in an image browser or image database, ideally at 100% magnification and in small groups side by side. The results shown here are my own created just as described. As I would have hoped after all these years, I can hold a camera steady at the reciprocal of the focal length, and that's practice and experience more than anything else. It could still do with some improvement, and it occurred to me that I haven't been following my own advice as much as I could. Nevertheless, that's my benchmark, the speed at which I would expect to get every frame sharp. Slower than this, however, the figures become more complicated. Here, it's useful to grade the degree of sharpness. Exact measurements, such as pixel smear, are irrelevant, as sharpness is ultimately perceptual. You do need to use your own judgment. I find the following categories, which are entirely personal, to be useful:

Extremely sharp	Significant motion blur
Acceptably sharp	Extreme motion blur
Slight motion blur	

The results are shown in Table 1. On the face of it, there seems to be a reasonably clear separation, with the results from the three slowest shutter speeds quite useless. However, the interesting speed is the one immediately below my benchmark speed, where one of the three was acceptable.

So, on to the next stage of the test, to get a better sampling by shooting more frames in quick succession I took 20 consecutive frames at my benchmark speed, 1/focal length, or in the case of this 85 mm lens, 1/80 sec. The result was that only a third of the frames were perfectly sharp, just over a half were acceptable, and a few were blurred. I followed this with another 20, at 2/focal length, or 1/40 sec, and finally 20 at 4/focal length, or 1/20 sec. The results in Table 2 show that there is no sharp dividing line between the lowest reliable shutter speed and the ones afflicted by shake. Instead, at the speeds below the benchmark, there is a percentage success rate. Moreover, even 1/20 sec, which would be foolhardy to try with any expectations, actually did deliver two acceptable frames out of 20. What we can learn from all this is first that over-shooting at certain speeds increases the probability of a sharp, usable frame; and second that the goal of training and practice is not just to improve your slowest reliable speed, but to improve the percentage success rate at all speeds.

How to improve these figures? First you need to know exactly what you are trying to correct and improve. Although this is a personal interpretation, four things cause camera shake, and each calls for different corrective techniques. These are drift, shaking, twitching, and jerking the shutter release. The first is a relatively slow movement around the subject caused mainly by the difficulty of concentrating absolutely on one thing for a period of time, and is entirely

Test procedure
This table indicates the camera settings you should shoot test frames at.

TEST PROCEDURE

Reference frame	Basic standard	1 stop over standard	2 stops over standard	3 stops over standard	4 stops over standard
1/2(focal length)	1/focal length	2/focal length	4/focal length	8/focal length	16/focal length
eg 1/200 sec. 100 mm	eg 1/100 sec. 100mm	eg 1/50 sec. 100 mm	eg 1/25 sec. 100 mm	eg 1/12 sec. 100 mm	eg 1/6 sec 100 mm
3 frames	3 frames	3 frames	3 frames	3 frames	3 frames

HAND HELD

Motion blur comparison

It is useful to use a program that allows you to compare the same region of multiple images at once, and see a 100% magnification.

natural. However, it becomes important in photography only when some precise alignment needs to be made, such as the edge of a subject very close to the frame edge. Shaking is connected to heart rate, breathlessness, and the general level of nervous energy. This is promoted by adrenalin, so being excited about a shot you are about to take is unhelpful, even though difficult to control. Twitching is also related to nervous energy, but is a much more distinct and jerking movement cause by muscle contraction. In the context of aiming at a target it is more likely to be semi-voluntary than involuntary. Semi-voluntary means that you are conscious that it is about

to happen because your brain is about to trigger the response, but that the tension caused by thinking about it, and by thinking about holding steady in general, seems to make it happen anyway. Finally, pressing down too hard on the shutter release does what you might expect, when all that is needed is a gentle squeeze.

People vary in how much they are prone to each of these, for physiological as well as psychological reason. Drift is the least problematical, and can usually be solved by full concentration and by not trying to hold the subject in the viewfinder for too long. As for the minor tremors of shaking, some people are by nature calmer and steadier than others, but ways of improving this include any number of ways of relaxing and slowing the heart rate, such as by deep breathing. Taking a deep breath, then slowly and steadily exhaling, and squeezing the shutter release at the end of this cycle is one reliable technique borrowed from target shooting. Another is to move onto a subject by either raising or lowering the camera, in order to take advantage of the steadying effect of motion. Twitches perversely tend to increase or are encouraged by the tension of trying to hold steady. One answer is to time the shot between two twitches, another is to raise the camera and shoot with as little delay as possible, trading accuracy in composition for steadiness. As you can see, there are a number of different approaches, and people tend to choose the one that suits their personality best.

TABLE 1 RESULTS
85MM LENS HAND-HELD, 3 FRAMES EACH SPEED

	1/160 sec	1/80 sec	1/40 sec	1/20 sec	1/10 sec	1/5 sec
Extremely sharp	3	3				
Acceptably sharp			1			
Slight motion blur			2			
Significant motion blur				1	1	
Extreme motion blur				2	2	3

TABLE 2 RESULTS
85MM LENS HAND-HELD, 20 FRAMES EACH SPEED

	1/80 sec	1/40 sec	1/20 sec
Extremely sharp	6	2	
Acceptably sharp	11	3	2
Slight motion blur	3	7	4
Significant motion blur		8	5
Extreme motion blur			9

STEADYING TECHNIQUES

STEADYING TECHNIQUES

It should go without saying that if there is a convenient support in the right place that you can use without wasting any time, use it. Photography isn't a sport and you don't get points for doing things the hard way. Ad hoc supports are where you find them, from the top of a low wall to a streetlight or the hood of a car. A piece of cloth or anything a little soft between the camera and the surface helps to dampen vibrations, as explained on the following pages. A soft camera bag can usually be made to work as a support; shape it to suit and press the camera and lens down onto it.

Perhaps most important of all is how you position your body and hold the camera. Stabilizing the body follows simple principles of mechanics, including holding the camera over your center of gravity and placing your feet somewhat apart at different angles (to more nearly oppose the axes of easiest rotation).

In addition, there are a number of ways of bracing your hands or arms against your body, and bracing your body against something solid. Crouching on one knee while resting one elbow on the raised knee is one method. A squatting position with ankles crossed just in front of you allows the raised bent knees to support both elbows. Lying prone with elbows on the ground will not appeal to anyone concerned about their clothes, but is probably the most stable body-only braced position.

That said, there are limits to the usefulness of shooting steadily at slow speeds, and these are set by the subject. If you can hold steady with a particular focal length at 1/15 sec, for example, this will not get you a sharp image if you are photographing a walking figure that almost fills the frame. The relative movement of things in the frame is an absolute limit for the shutter speed—if, of course, absolute sharpness is important to you.

No support
The weight rests on both elbows. Place left hand far forward.

HOLDING THE CAMERA

VARIOUS HAND POSITIONS
The hand positions illustrated here are aimed to maximize the steadiness of the camera while still leaving access to the controls unfettered. The latter can be especially important in rapidly changing conditions.

Horizontal grip
The weight of the camera is distributed equally between the hands.

STANCE
As important to a lowlight photographer as to a marksman or archer, body and arm position is critical. If possible, use any available support.

Supports
Leaning against a wall or tree can help. If necessary use a jacket as a cushion.

AD HOC SUPPORTS & TELEPHOTOS
Rigidity is more important with a long-focus lens than with any other. Not only is the image magnified, but also the shake, as illustrated on page 73.

Available support
A camera bag or other object gives a three point support.

Horizontal grip, side view
Press both elbows into your chest to reduce muscular strain and improve steadiness.

Battery grip, horizontal
Use the additional hand grip on the battery attachment if there is one. Left hand is free to operate lens.

Vertical grip
The left hand takes the weight of the camera.

Alternative vertical grip
Reversing the vertical grip is more awkward, although the left hand is more free.

Battery pack, vertical
Bulky battery packs are more difficult to use vertically. Take more weight in right hand.

Standing posture
Spread your weight between both feet, placing one slightly in front of the other. Attempt to find as relaxed and balanced a stance as possible, with your hand grip as shown above.

Kneeling
This is a more stable solution than standing, but admittedly less convenient. Rest on your heel and support your left elbow on your knee, making a solid camera rest.

Squatting
In this position you can form a camera platform with your body. Rest your elbows on your knees and lean forward, forming a compact, relaxed structure.

Ground level
Rest the camera directly on the ground, or on a bean bag on the ground. Take a test shot and review on the LCD.

Above your head
To see over crowds, guess the composition and shoot. Review on the LCD.

Side grip, motor drive
Gripping the lens mount from the side is more stable, but manual focusing is tricky.

Overhand horizontal
An overhand grip on the lens mount helps pull it back firmly against your face for support.

Underhand horizontal
Press your left elbow firmly into your chest, supporting the lens weight from below.

Overhand vertical
Very little adjustment is needed from the horizontal stance.

Underhand vertical, battery grip
The extra bulk makes the right arm less stable.

Underhand, battery grip
The weight is supported by the left hand and leg, the right is free to operate camera.

Squatting, battery grip horizontal
Both hands take the strain, passing it via the elbows to the knees. Ankles are crossed.

Available support
If possible, use any available surface to support the camera. A camera bag can often add extra height or padding.

STEADYING EQUIPMENT

There are a number of small, light devices which, while falling short of the complete stability possible from a tripod, can fit into the hand held style of photography and offer instant support.

The idea of hand held shooting, as just discussed, is the freedom to do without a tripod, with its added bulk and slow set-up. Nevertheless, just as the camera can quickly be steadied against a part of the body, there are various supports, mostly small, that can be brought into use quickly and easily without compromising the freedom to move and shoot. The tradeoff between stability on the one hand and lightness and ease of setting up on the other is here skewed heavily towards the latter.

One of the disadvantages of all mounts in this kind of shooting is the time it takes to attach the camera (or lens), and some kind of quick-release plate is important. An L-shaped plate, as shown opposite, allows the camera to be mounted for vertical as well as horizontal format, and when speed is essential this scores strongly over plates that attach the base of the camera only.

Monopods are a long-established design of fast support, and can be used either free-standing for an improvement in the order of a couple of stops, or wedged or propped against something solid for more stability. A ball-and-socket head, which can be used slightly loosened, is probably the most useful mount.

Miniature tripods, also known as mini-pods, have the advantage of being small enough to fit into the side pocket of a shoulder bag, or even a trouser pocket. There are several ingenious designs and this kind of tripod works well braced against a wall or any vertical surface, and when the legs are folded together it can be also used as a hand grip.

The camera can be further steadied by applying either compression or tension. Compression typically means pressing the camera against a surface or a part of the body, and this is effective also with a mini-tripod. Miniature supports like this are light in weight and resist torque poorly, so if the camera is left more or less free on the mount, it is quite likely to suffer some camera shake from mirror slap. We'll go into this in more detail when we look at regular tripods on pages 160-163. Pressing down on the camera with one hand, or even placing a jacket or shoulder bag on it, improves steadiness. Without a miniature support, an important precaution when resting the camera on a hard surface is to place something slightly soft underneath—a piece of clothing, for example. This will dampen any vibrations from your body or from the mirror.

Tension is the opposite of compression, and equally effective, although it is a little more difficult to put into practice. Essentially, tension needs a strap of some kind. The tension strap, works like a monopod in reverse: one foot secures the base of the strap while you pull the camera upwards to tension it. Even the regular camera strap can be put to use, by placing it against something solid and then leaning backwards to tension the strap. This means first composing and then shooting blind, briefly, but works if the camera is places between railings, for example. In all of this, some improvisation is called for.

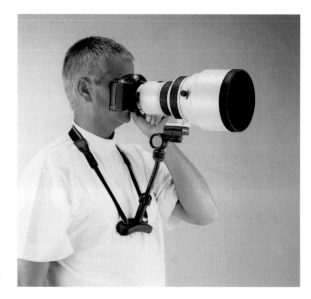

Pistock C
Novoflex chest and shoulder pod used with a neck strap to transfer the weight from a heavy fast telephoto to the chest.

KIT BAG

Depending on the situation, there are a number of tools you can call upon to steady your shooting.

Chest pod
A folding chest pod transfers the camera weight from the arms to the body. With sliding column, quick release ball head and quick release coupling system.

Tension strap
From Kirk. Can be used on it's own, or to pull a monopod against.

Monopod
Allows you to rest the camera weight on the ground but move fast.

Mini tripod
Allows you to place the camera on objects.

Novoflex rods
You can build light and flexible supports for different situations from a modular set of rods and brackets.

fixed rods

MB Grip
Handle screws into tripod socket.

long flexible rod

Telesack
A leather bag filled with dried beans, capable of suppressing vibrations. A useful quick support, especially with long lenses.

flexible rod

bracket fittings

Shoulder brace
A shoulder brace works in a way similar to a gunstock. Pulling back on the front grip transfers even more weight onto the shoulder.

brackets

rod

Pistock
Versatile chest and shoulder pod design from Novoflex.

Longer

Shorter

Micropod
Small tripod for lightweight cameras.

Flash Grip
A large handle attached to the tripod socket.

KIT BAG (CONTINUED)

Following on from page 79, here are some more items to consider adding to your kit bag.

Bean bag
Kinesis bean bag "shell" filled with either 2.7 kg of polyethylene beads or 0.7 kg of buckwheat. With two compartments it can be folded for additional height, as shown.

Panning plate
From Kinesis. Fitted with a quick-release plate, its broad frame gives extra stability for panning when used on top of a bean bag, jacket or any improvised soft support.

Bladders
Water bladder (left) and sand bladder (right), here both empty, can be used to make a "bean bag" camera support from on-site materials.

Culman monopod
A high load capacity (3.5 kg) suitable for telephoto lenses, and a jointed rubber foot that allows it to be rotated and tilted while still in full contact with the ground.

Culman Monofix
A monopod with a ball head, hand loop, and nine sections that folds to 30 cm and extends to 142 cm.

Caullman mini tripod
Folds down to a very compact size.

Caption head
Novoflex BasicBall fitted with three telescope rods.

Monopods
With stylish detachable safety cap.

Novoflex BasicBall
Fitted with three short ball-tipped rods.

Novoflex Microstativ
A simple table-top design without attachments.

Ball head
Can be attached to tripods like those to the left.

Novoflex Microstativ
A simple table-top design with small ball head.

Novoflex Minipod
Offers high stability combined with unusual flexibility, achieved by the individually variable angle at which each of the legs can be set. There are preset positions at angles of 30°, 60°, and 90° and it can support equipment weighing up to 22 lbs (10 kg).

Zip bean bag
Bean bag from Kinesis features a zippered compartment, so that the fill can be dumped directly inside without the need for a liner.

Novoflex forked joint
Even without mounting to a tripod it offers quick, valuable steadying, especially for a long lens.

Forked joint and clamp
Novoflex forked joint attached to a clamp. Highly portable.

Poly husk beads
Standard recommended fill for bean bags - polyethylene beads on the left, buckwheat on the right. The polyethylene is much heavier, but more solid as a support.

STEADYING EQUIPMENT

STABILIZING TECHNOLOGY

Under the names Image Stabilization (Canon) and Vibration Reduction (Nikon), this lens technology, invented in the mid-90s, is spectacularly useful in lowlight photography. The basic principle is straightforward, the execution less so. Camera shake—that is the inability to hold the image steady at slow speeds—results in the focused image moving rapidly on a plane perpendicular to the camera axis. If the lens, or one of its elements, can be made to move in exactly the opposite direction to the shake, the image will be stabilized.

Fast-response circuitry and micromotors built into the lens have added a new and very valuable dimension to steadying the image, and can improve shake-free shooting speeds by up to 3 to 5 stops.

In practice, the special lens is equipped with sensors that can detect the movement, and a microprocessor to analyze it and transmit the necessary information to micromotors. The Nikon VR system, for which there is more published information available, is contained in a unit that contains a floating lens element within the lens assembly. Handheld camera shake takes place on two axes, pitch (up and down) and yaw (side to side), also known as the x and y axes respectively (the z axis, roll, is irrelevant here). Two angular velocity sensors, one for each axis, detect movement and are sampled every 1/1000 second. This data is sent to a microcomputer built into the lens, and from their combined reading, the angular velocity is known for any direction across the plane. The microcomputer calculates the compensation needed in direction and strength, and transmits this to two voice coil motors, one to move the lens element horizontally, the other vertically. (Voice coil motors, or VCM, were originally developed for speaker systems and are wire coils used to move a component back and forth within a magnetic field.) Working together, and controlled by the electric current within the unit's magnetic field, they compensate for any motion in the vertical plane.

In most cases, the system is activated by lightly pressing the shutter release. As the shutter is pressed for shooting, the motors engage and the viewfinder image jitters as the compensatory movements are made. In the Nikon system, the floating element is centered immediately before exposure so as to allow the most efficient compensation. Canon and Nikon systems vary in how and when this compensation is displayed, and while many photographers find the jittering distracting, it gives a valuable indication of when the compensation has been fully made (the jittering stops). Added sophistications are algorithms for when the camera is mounted on a tripod (camera shake can happen at shutter speeds around from 1/30 sec to half a second because of mirror slap on an SLR) and for deliberate panning. Panning recognition works by sensing gross horizontal movements and discounting them.

Moving lens element stabilization
The lens element in the third example has moved to compensate for the vibration. The yellow line represents the image, which is directed more successfully than the non-stablized second arrangement.

Stabilizing lenses
Nikon (above) and Canon (right) build image stabilization technology into some of their lenses, like these.

On/ off switch
Both Canon and Nikon versions of the technology can be switched on or off using a switch on the lens. If the stabilizer is built into the camera, the switch is likely to be on the camera body instead.

Moving sensor stabilization
This is the "Super Steady Shot" mechanism featured in the Sony α700, that moves the sensor to compensate for camera shake. Sony claims this delivers a 4-stop advantage over non-stabilized systems.

Sony α700
Sony has continued the tradition of the line of cameras bought from Konica-Minolta which include moving-sensor stabilization.

STABILIZING TECHNOLOGY

The improvements over non-stabilized hand-holding are in the order of 3 to 5 stops, and the greatest benefit is at longer focal lengths. This does, however, depend on the photographer's success at holding a camera steady in the first place. Nikon studies with a 200 mm lens show that a photographer who can achieve a 70% success rate unstabilized at 1/125 sec can expect the same results stabilized at 1/15 sec. Stabilized lenses demand power, although the systems contain means to conserve this. Tests show an average draw of 80 microamps when activated (but not functioning), which is four times that of a digital SLR without stabilization.

A different approach was taken by Konica-Minolta in their Maxxum 7D DSLR, in which the sensor moves to compensate for the shake. The CCD sensor is mounted on a movable platform that can be shifted in the x and y axes by actuators. The considerable advantage of this is that it works with all lenses, including old ones. This was first introduced in the DiMage A1 digital camera, for which Konica-Minolta claimed that "when using the camera at the telephoto setting (an equivalent focal length of 200 mm), approximately 90% of the images recorded will be sharp with a shutter speed of 1/25 second." Sony has continued developing the technology, and with the α700 the claimed improvement is up to 4 f-stops. There are disadvantages, however. One is the effect is not obvious through the viewfinder because the lens is not involved, meaning that you see no compensating judder or inertia, although a 5-step indicator in the viewfinder shows that the system is functioning. Opinion is divided, as just mentioned, but without the immediate evidence that the compensation is at work there is more of a need to stop and check the result on the LCD screen, which of course slows down shooting. The second disadvantage is that this in-body system is currently not quite as responsive as the in-lens technology, although this may well improve.

An older technology is gyroscopic stabilization, which is still used in cinematography. The principle is the conservation of angular momentum, achieved by two relatively heavy wheels spinning rapidly on two opposed axes. Kenyon Laboratories, for example, produce the KS-4 stabilizer, which is claimed to allow hand held shooting at 1 second, with gyros spinning at 22,000 rpm. This comes at the cost of weight and bulk though, as it weighs 2 lbs, before the power pack is attached, and measures 4.3 × 2.8 inches (11 × 7 cm).

Pitching and yawing
As this illustration shows, the most important movement that must be detected and combatted by an IS system is the pitch and yaw.

With versus without
This technology comes into its own at a certain band of shutter-speed-times-focal-length—the few stops below which you can reasonably expect to hold steady without assistance. In this test, I used a 300 mm efl hand-held at 1/13 sec. Out of 6 frames with and without vibration reduction, all but one with VR on were sharp, while all but one with VR off were distinctly shaken.

FAST LENSES

Prime lenses (that is, those with a fixed focal length) used to be the standard for professional photography, until their status was gradually eroded by zoom lenses with excellent optical qualities and remarkable zoom ranges. Yet one of the advantages of prime lenses is that they can be designed with very wide maximum apertures. This is not new technology, and ultra-fast lenses, from the early Ermanox from 1924 with its Emostar $f1.8$ (not great by today's standards but remarkable then) to the Canon 50 mm $f0.95$ lens of the 1960s and the Noct-Nikkor $f1.2$ are a part of camera history. Extremely high resolution is a necessity, because, as we'll see on the following pages, a large maximum aperture results in shallow depth of field, and this usually concentrates the focus on a tiny area, making its definition all the more crucial. The main problem for most people is the cost; good, fast primes are very expensive. Other issues are that they tend to be relatively bulky and heavy, a consequence of all that extra glass, and many,

While zoom lenses have got ever-better, this is usually at the cost of maximum apertures. Lowlight photography argues for dedicated fast prime lenses.

surprisingly, have manual rather than automatic focus. The decision to invest in a fast lens for lowlight shooting largely rests on how much of this kind of photography you intend to do. The performance advantage, however, can be considerable. Of course, unlike film photography, where the bottom line was the amount of light entering through the lens, digital shooting allows quick changes to the ISO. Nevertheless, a fast lens allows you to hold off the moment at which you dial up the sensitivity and start to lose image quality to noise.

What counts as fast in a lens? Always, of course, the faster the better, but in the context of modern lenses, the maximum aperture should be greater than $f2$. The fractional numbers at this end of the aperture scale belie the actual differences. A lens of $f1.4$ captures twice as much light as $f2$, and four times as much as a "regular" $f2.8$ lens. The cost of doing this is considerable in terms of precision, type of glass, weight, bulk, and money. Hidden issues are the aberrations and edge performance failings that appear at very wide apertures. Nikon's 58 mm Noct-Nikkor, for example, was designed especially to overcome sagittal coma, in which point sources of light appear crescent-shaped (or, as Nikon charmingly put it, like "a bird spreading its wings"). This aberration, disastrous for city lights and stars, disappears when the lens is stopped down just slightly, but to correct it for wide-open use the front element was ground aspherically, and high refractive glass was used to allow all the elements to have shallower curvatures.

Wide maximum apertures at extreme focal lengths are even more difficult to manufacture, and practically this restricts the choice of fast lenses to focal lengths not far from standard. The range from 35mm to 85mm is the norm. With a fast lens being a considerable investment, deciding which is important. The arguments for a wider angle are coverage and less risk of camera shake (as there is less movement of the image in the frame at a wider angle), but a possible disadvantage is that wide-angle views are generally, through familiarity, expected to be more or less sharp throughout the scene. The arguments for medium

Lights detail
This details shows the lights from the photograph opposite. Taken with a 58mm Noct-Nikkor lens at full aperture (f1.2) there is no sign of any coma "tail." The radial flare around the various lamps is pronounced, but pleasant.

Sagittal coma

This disturbing blur shape, noticeable in sharp focus and even more so with soft focus, is a distortion effect that fast lenses are computed to avoid. The example here is particularly bad, with a slow wide-angle lens at close to full aperture—f 5.6. Note that the coma "points" towards the center of the lens and is at its worst close to the edges of the field.

Building detail

Building detail

telephoto are that it makes a perfect lowlight portrait lens, and that the strongly blurred out-of-focus areas can enhance the sharpness of the focused zone; against this, coverage is restricted and camera shake more likely. We deal with focusing issues in more detail on the following pages.

FAST LENSES

The quality of the unfocused areas in the image, sometimes referred to by the Japanese word "bokeh" (ぼけ), varies between lenses, and in the case of a fast prime from a good manufacturer, considerable care goes into this aspect. In these two side-by-side comparisons between a Zeiss 85 mm Planar and a Nikon 24-120 mm zoom, a detailed 100% view is revealing. The image below, seen in full view, is of a slate wall shot from an extreme angle for the purposes of this demonstration. The apertures have been kept identical. In both cases, the results are masked to an

extent by the superior resolution of the Zeiss, which emphasizes the transition from sharp to unfocused. At *f*5.6 — the minimum aperture for the Nikon zoom — the transition to blur is clearly more distinct with the Zeiss, and the blurring is smoother. Note that the Nikon's soft areas show signs of a kind of artifacting in the form of edges being retained. I say artifacting because in the detailed blow-up of one of the small shadow areas, you can see that the suggestion of vertical edges in the *f*5.6 version turns out to be false in the less-blurred *f*16 image.

Zeiss v Nikon *f*5.6

Zeiss v Nikon *f*16

HAND HELD

Zeiss 85 mm *f*1.4

Zeiss 85 mm *f*5.6

Zeiss 85 mm *f*16

Nikon 24-120 mm *f*5.6

Nikon 24-120 mm *f*16

Highlight issues

Depending on taste, fast lenses at full aperture may have drawbacks. In these two photographs of a fishing boat at night, taken within a short time of each other, one with a fast Zeiss f1.4 lens, the other Nikon 18-200mm zoom, the powerful tungsten lamps hung out from the sides of the vessel to attract squid are rendered very differently. The treatment from the Zeiss lens is much less realistic.

Zeiss 85mm

Nikon 24-120mm

Nikon blur artifacting

Notice the small shadow areas indicated.

AF Nikkor 85 mm

Leica Noctilux-M 50 mm

Canon f1.0L 50 mm

Canon f1.2L USM

Voigtlander 35/1.2 Nokton Aspherical

Zeiss 85mm f1.4 ZF Planar T

A SELECTION OF FAST LENSES

	max f stop	notable feature
Canon 50mm f0.95	f0.95	Fastest production lens for a 35mm ever (made 1960)
Canon 50mm f1.0L USM	f1.0	Fastest current SLR lens, heavy
AF Nikkor 85mm	f1.4D IF	Portrait focal length, autofocus
Canon EF 85mm f1.2L USM	f1.2	Very fast portrait lens, autofocus
Zeiss 85mm f1.4 ZF Planar T*	f1.4	A traditional 6-element design delivering an exceptionally flat image plane Nikon, Pentax and Fujifilm SLR it, manual focus
Leica Noctilux-M 50 mm f1.0	f1.4	A legendary lens, re-markable for its lack of flare. Fastest current rangefinder lens
Voigtlander 35/1.2 Nokton Aspherical	f1.2	Leica fit. A moderately priced alternative to the Noctilux
Voigtlander Nokton 58mm f1.4 SLII	f1.4	Moderately priced, Nikon and Pentax SLR fit

FOCUS AT FULL APERTURE

When composition and camera viewpoint permit, one standard method of maximizing the shallow depth of field at full aperture is to shoot so perpendicular to the main axis of the subject. In the case of this mantis, the length of the insect obviously makes this worthwhile.

I f you are used to the forgiving focusing range of a normal lens (and these days, full aperture on many zooms is $f3.5 - f5.6$) then working to precision with a fast lens wide open can come as a shock. For example, on my Nikon D2X, using a Zeiss 85 mm Planar at $f1.4$ and focusing on a subject at 16.4 ft (5 m), the depth of field is around 7.4 in (19 cm). Compare this with the 30 in (77 cm) when the lens is stopped down to $f5.6$. Depth of field is at best a fuzzy concept, and the calculations are not to be taken literally as it is ultimately based on the concept of "sharp enough," involving both judgment and the definition of the circle of confusion. The circle of confusion is the smallest diameter that an imaged point can be and still look like a point (see box on following pages). If your eyesight is good, and you are examining the final photograph closely and critically, the outer limits of this depth of field may not satisfy you. This, as you might expect, tends to happen with photographers investing in and using one of these costly lenses.

Extremely shallow depth of field and dim light make special demands on the normally simple act of focusing, including targeting the focus.

COMPARE FOCUS

With the camera steadied to avoid the risk, focus at full aperture with a long focal length (here 85 mm at $f1.4$) on a subject containing sharp detail, in this case the metal grille of an audio speaker. Using manual focus, or manual focus override, take a series of frames with very slight differences in focus—though all should be visually sharp through the viewfinder. The focus indicator in the viewfinder will also help in this. Here, examining the frames together at 100% shows the slight focus shift, although at the time of shooting any of these would have seemed correct. For the purposes of this demonstration, I chose this speaker grille because of its slight curvature, and marked the sharp focus point with arrows.

In almost all short to medium-distance scenes, only a very small part of the image can be sharply focused at a wide aperture. This is even more pronounced if you use a medium telephoto portrait lens. Basically, depth of field is not an option, and there is usually no point in trying to maximize it. The only strategy worth pursuing to get more than one point in the image sharp is alignment—re-positioning yourself or some objects in the scene so that they are at the same distance.

Typically, however, the first consideration is identifying the exact part of the image on which to focus. Usually this is obvious, though not always, and there may be a conflict of choice, as in the example opposite. Having decided, be careful when relying on the autofocus to deliver the best result. As the image illustrates, in a deep area of the scene it is easy for the focus to be slightly, but significantly, out.

The problem is compounded greatly with manual focusing. As you may have noticed from the table on the previous pages, some modern fast lenses are still made without autofocus, yet why would a reportage photographer deliberately make life difficult by buying one of these. I can answer this question personally, as my last lens purchase was the Zeiss 85mm *f* 1.4 Planar just mentioned, even though I might have chosen the Nikon model for around the same price, with the same focal length, same maximum aperture, but with autofocus, which you might think essential in getting the focus exactly right. In many cases, it is faster and more accurate than manual focus, but it depends on the subject, and in lowlight photography, as we've seen, images can easily confuse automated systems of all kinds. Specular highlights and large dense areas of shadow can easily throw autofocus, with the added risk of your shooting without realizing this. Manual focus, while slower, gives more personal control, and the focusing indicators in the viewfinder frame are particularly helpful. But a more important reason is that fast lens design is at the specialized, craftsmanlike end of lens manufacture, and much attention is paid to the subtle qualities of out-of-focus appearance, contrast, and general, idiosyncratic feel, in addition to build quality. These lenses are not at the heart of mass-production, and so can be treated differently. The Zeiss lens, for example, is a Planar, which means it is optimized for a flat field across the frame.

One technique, which takes up more time, but helps guarantee the result, is to shoot extra frames with very slight shifts to the framing and the autofocus on. This slight re-framing will give you a range of sharp-focus points from which to choose later. Another precaution, which also delays shooting, is to set aside several seconds to examine the image at magnification on the LCD screen. Obviously, doing either of these depends on the kind of subject—one that is not changing or moving very much.

WHERE TO FOCUS

All kinds of detailed decisions are involved in where to focus whenever there is choice. In the case of this museum shot with a medium telephoto, slight adjustments to framing and the movement of the people in shot gave two possibilities. The basic framing is trying to juxtapose the paintings of standing women with real visitors, but full depth of field is impossible. In the first shot, the woman in the middle distance seems to be the natural focus of attention, but in the second, the action of the woman in the distance, holding up a camera and framed more neatly against the strip of white wall, shifts the attention to her, and so I shifted the focus to her also.

Comparison
This comparison makes it easy to see the two focus points—check the well-defined belt buckle and bag strap.

Range of sharpness
The gradual shift from sharply focused to unfocused across the plane of the image is often no bad thing, and the blurring can be attractive, particularly if it creates a kind of color wash. All that's needed is to focus on a logical point, of which there may be several. Here, with a glass restaurant wall, the first letter of the name is the logical choice.

DEFINING SHARPNESS

Sharpness is almost always critical in lowlight photography, simply because the technical limits of depth of field and shutter speed are constantly being pushed. First, however, it's important to understand that sharpness is subjective, an overall, personal assessment from a combination of factors which can include the resolution of the lens, the focus, noise, contrast, motion blur, and how closely someone examines the image. Most of the time in photography, sharpness is an ideal, or at least a desirable quality, but by no means always. There may well be other qualities that override the importance of sharpness. Consider a shot that captures a particular gesture elegantly but is ever so slightly less sharp in some respect than the following frame; yet the second frame is not quite so well timed. The content may well tip the balance towards the first. And in case we get too fixated on sharpness, let's recall Henri Cartier-Bresson's comment: "I am constantly amused by... an insatiable craving for sharpness of images. Is this the passion of an obsession?... Do these people hope... to get closer to grips with reality?"

> **Sharpness is a subjective impression, not technical, and because of this it is affected by several lowlight issues, each with different effects.**

A useful exercise is to make test shots whenever there is time, in advance of an important shot, and check them on the LCD screen at full magnification. Lettering of any kind, such as signs or vehicle number plates, is a good subject; the idea is to become familiar with what is an acceptable sharpness. It is very common when editing a lowlight shoot to find a proportion of images slightly unsharp for one reason or another (wrong focus point, subject movement, camera shake). Because these technical issues cannot be taken for granted in this kind of photography, editing takes longer. When examining the images in a browser or database, each one needs to viewed at high magnification—full size or three-quarter size. Beware when deleting images not to throw away those that may have some use when repaired.

An important perceptual consideration is that wide-aperture shooting creates two different textures in the image, equally important. One is the small in-focus area, the other the surrounding, usually much larger areas that are out of focus. The quality and "feel" of these out of focus zones makes an important contribution, and is the reason why many photographers tend to be partisan about specific lenses. Lens designers do indeed work towards a particular style of "out of focusness," particularly with fast lenses. Not only are the out of focus zones important in their own right, but perceptually they contribute to the concentration of sharpness in the small focused details. Compositional techniques such as positioning a small sharp area against the extreme blur of a strongly defocused background aid the impression of sharpness.

Key sharp detail

For perceptual reasons, as long as one key detail in the image is sharp, the eye and brain accept and assume a greater sense of overall sharpness than may, in fact, exist. Here, a telephoto shot of men in a Burmese temple is sharply focused only on the eyebrow-to-chin profile of the further man and on the tobacco smoke he is exhaling. This is enough, however, to give a satisfactory general impression of sharpness.

Sharpness also needs to be considered in the context of digital sharpening, which we deal with shortly. At some point before final output, all digital images need sharpening, because of the way they are captured, which introduces some softness, and because of the characteristics of the printer or other output device, so that the final image has the desired crispness and sparkle. These standard needs are not always easy to distinguish from the more localized and personal issues, such as repairing or enhancing details in an image which were not focused or frozen adequately—which happens frequently in lowlight photography. On the following pages we'll look at this as a separate sharpening procedure.

Stopping down from the maximum aperture is clearly one way of reducing the risk of imperfect focusing, but the cost is the noise from racking up the ISO—negating the very reason, of course, for using a fast lens. Nevertheless, this is one of the possible trade-offs discussed earlier, on pages 18-19.

Sharpness from flash
The technique of rear-curtain flash in combination with a slow shutter speed delivers a different quality of sharpness from normal. The flash at the end of the exposure adds an overlay of sharpness in just some elements over a base of blurred movement.

Using composition
Careful composition can sometimes make shallow focus a positive feature. Here, three macaw feathers are lit and positioned in such a way that the sharply focused edge of the nearest blue feather is set against a soft shadow that matches its position, and so enhances it.

DEPTH OF FIELD AT WIDE APERTURES

Depth of field is the distance between the nearest and farthest points in a subject that appear acceptably sharp in an image. The smaller the lens aperture, the greater the depth of field. It is ultimately subjective, and influenced by the following:-

- Focal length
- Circle of confusion
- Aperture
- Viewing distance of final image
- Subject distance

When slightly out of focus, a point is imaged as a tiny circle. The circle of confusion (CoC) is the smallest that this circle can be and still appear sharp to the eye at a normal viewing distance. This is subjective, but most lens

manufacturers work to between 0.025 mm and 0.033 mm for a 24 × 26 mm frame (that of 35 mm film). Smaller sensors call for a smaller CoC.

Depth of field calculators are available online. The one used for the calculations here is:

http://www.dofmaster.com/dofjs.html

Depth of field
These berries are in sharp focus, but the high aperture means that closer foreground (the leaf) and background are not in focus.

THE TECHNICAL EDIT

In normal, bright-light, or flash photography, you might go straight to image selection on aesthetic grounds, on the reasonable assumption that the images will be technically competent. Any serious issues, such as auto-focus incorrectly targeted on the background instead of the subject, would have flagged themselves at the time of shooting. Not so in lowlight photography, and particularly not so with hand-held. As already discussed, the combination of shutter speed, aperture, and ISO setting is, for much of the shoot, likely to put you on the edge of acceptability.

Because uncertainty over sharpness and other errors is a basic fact of lowlight photography, a technical quality check is the first essential step in the workflow.

Whichever browser, database or workflow program you use for selecting which images to process, the very first step is to check for sharpness, while also keeping an eye on the worst effects of noise. Sharpness, as we've seen, is more complex than it at first seems, and involves a heavy dose of personal judgment; grounds for rejection are generally poor focus, camera shake, and subject motion blur. At a finer level there are your own standards for what you consider truly sharp as opposed to "just" sharp, and the expressions "pin-sharp" and "tack-sharp" spring to mind. More complex is deciding between images in which the point of sharp focus varies, and this becomes more of an issue with wide apertures and longer focal lengths. In the case of the jackal picture here, shot at $f4$ with a 600 mm lens (900 mm equivalent on the Nikon camera used), the depth of field is remarkably shallow, such that either the whiskers or the eyes could be truly sharp, but not both.

As one of the key strategies for hand-held shooting at slow shutter speeds is to spread the risk by taking several-to-many frames, you will often have a sequence of very similarly composed images, and this helps the technical check enormously — provided that the software you use for selection allows them to be ranged alongside each other on the screen for a detail side-by-side comparison. The software packages here show the various alternatives, with some clearly better at comparative display than others.

Opinions vary on what to do once you've made a judgment. There are three technical categories possible: unacceptable, acceptable, and best. Some photographers prefer to bin the clearly flawed images, but given that some repair may be possible, there are valid arguments for simply tagging them and keeping them. It's also worth bearing in mind that future software my be able to achieve more effective repair than at present. Added to this are creative or aesthetic judgments touched upon already, such as preferring the composition of one frame which may not be the absolute sharpest, but which is still acceptable technically.

HAND HELD

DxO Optics Pro
A four-up display in the Organize section of the workflow can be zoomed in on equally.

CAPTURE ONE

The comparison feature allows a 2-up or 4-up display portrait or landscape, with a focus tool that displays a detail of one image in a small window and the effect of applying an Unsharp Mask. This last feature may or may not be helpful. On the one hand, it enables you to set a sharpness benchmark, but on the other this is digital edge sharpening, which has little to do with the quality of the original image.

Lightroom
Here Lightroom is shown in comparison mode. When one picture is being viewed, simply click anywhere to zoom the view to 100%.

Aperture
Aperture has a built in loupe which can be called up and dismissed by simply pressing the "~" (tilde) key. The zoom ratio defaults to 100%, but can be adjusted.

IVIEW

TAGGING WITH LABELS

One procedure is to assign label colors to images according to the way you work. In this example, using Expression Media, I have one warning label identifying flawed images, and another identifying the best (in my opinion) of a sequence.

Label	
None	0
First Selects	1
Second selects	2
Best of sequence	3
Flawed (usually focus or shake)	4
First of stitch sequence	5
Middle of stitch sequence	6
Last of stitch sequence	7
Single-shot HDR sequence	8
	9

IVIEW MEDIAPRO The Lightbox feature of this software is one of the best for close side-by-side analysis, combining vertical or horizontal slices with a magnifying "loupe."

IDENTIFYING BLUR FOR REPAIR

Sharpness and varying degrees of blur play such a prominent part in lowlight photography that I'm dwelling on them at length, and in particular looking closely at what affects them. Partly this is to do with analyzing faults so that they can be corrected in future, and partly also because repairing them, when this is possible, call for slightly different techniques. There are two basic kinds of blur, which is to say two basic causes of unsharpness. One is focus blur, in which point sources in the subject reproduce not as points but as discs, and the other is motion blur, in which features in the subject that should be sharp in the image reproduce as streaks or smears. And there is every possibility that both kinds of blur appear combined.

Both for repair and for avoiding in future shooting, it's important to be able to distinguish between blur due to focus error and blur due to movement of camera or subject.

Let's first consider focus blur, which through familiarity tends to be the standard against which other varieties can be compared. As we saw on the previous pages, focus blurring increases steadily according to the depth of the scene away from the point of focus. Most scenes shot at a wide aperture, therefore, contain many different degrees of out-of-focusness.

Perhaps the key quality of focus blur is that each point becomes a circle. We already saw this on the previous pages when we examined circles of confusion and depth of field. In digital terms, each pixel becomes a circle of pixels centerd on the original point. This provides the basis for specialized image restoration software to work. As the blur is isotropic (equal in all directions), knowing the blur width helps in attempting to reverse the blur towards the original sharpness. Technically, it is the Point Spread Function (PSF) that defines the amount of spreading—that is, blurring. As we'll see on the following pages, unsharp masking, which is the standard procedure for most image sharpening, including in Photoshop, is not necessarily the ideal for repairing this kind of optical blur. A point to note here is that with a perfect lens (an impossibility), the PSF predicts a perfect circle, but in real life the blur shape is often different, if only slightly so. Sophisticated blur repair needs to take this into account, and as the examples on these pages show, blur shapes can differ. Unsharp masking, incidentally, assumes that the blur radially follows a Gaussian (bell-shaped) curve (see box on page 98).

The ideal feature in an image to use for identifying focus blur is a point which contrasts strongly with its setting, and the perfect example of this is a specular highlight. While it is impossible to predict or determine which bright points of light are indeed points and not circles to begin with, reflections of a light in a curved surface (sun on raindrops, distant electric lamp in spectacles) and refractions (light sparkling in jewelry) tend to be small enough in a typical image to have no measurable dimension. When sharply focused, these appear as points, but the more defocussed they are, the larger the diameter of disc they become, as the sequence here shows. More often, however, there are no such easy point-source clues, and you may have to fall back on other ways of examining the image. One telltale feature of focus blur will always be in the same perpendicular plane (the one exception being a tilt lens or bellows, which will tilt the plane of sharp focus according to the Scheimpflug Principle, but these are specialized equipment found normally on large-format cameras). Another clue is to find parts of the image that commonsense tells you are closer or further than other parts, and to look at magnified details to see if they differ in sharpness. This is the technique used in the image of the Burmese Buddha.

Finally, there is the heuristic approach, a fancy way of saying try out focus repair procedures to see if they have any effect. In the case of the program used on the following pages for repair, Focus Magic, this involves letting the software analyze details, and also alternating between focus blur repair and motion blur repair. This is a rough and ready method, but can work.

Unsharpness due to movement has special qualities that set it apart from defocussed blur, and it can be further subdivided into camera motion blur and subject motion blur.

BLUR SHAPES

Defocussed specular
The specular highlights of the sun in the rounded chrome-metal top to a simple stapler are ideal for a focus-blur test. The image is defocussed in stages, and the blur shape from a high-quality lens (a Zeiss Planar) stays circular. Not, however, that one of the characteristics of this very sharp lens is to create an annulus (outer ring) to the blur circle, in a color that derives from axial chromatic aberration.

Oblate vs streaked
The upper detail of candles in this scene appears here in two versions of blur. In one of the several frames actually shot, the flames are out of focus, and show flattened circles (oblate) that are typical of blur shapes close to the edge of lens coverage. In the other version, camera shake imparts a slightly wiggled vertical streak to the shape.

Distortion increasing with blur
Details from three separate exposures at different focus points made of the Pudong skyline from Shanghai, on a 28mm PC shift lens. The distortion, stretched towards the center of the lens' field of coverage, increases with the amount of defocussing.

Coma
Sagittal coma shows itself as a curved, stretched shape that points towards the center of the image, and is worst at wide apertures with wide-angle lenses near the edges of the frame, as in these two examples.

IDENTIFYING BLUR FOR REPAIR

Motion blur differs from focus blur in that it has direction, and if you know or can calculate this direction, it is easier to restore than focus blur. The effect is a kind of smearing. Here, though, it's important to distinguish between camera shake and subject motion blur. In the first, the entire image is smeared by the same amount because the camera rather than part of the subject has been moved during the exposure. Subject motion blur involves relative motion—one thing moving against a background, typically, such as a car along a street. This kind of relative motion is more difficult to restore than camera shake, because it needs different amounts of correction across the frame.

There are further sub-divisions, and ultimately a wide variety of motion blur images. Camera shake involves both time and direction; the longer the exposure, the longer the streaks will be. Deliberate motion blur by moving the camera often involves changes of direction. A special case, more relevant to tripod shooting, is a medium-long exposure in which the camera shake, whether from mirror slap or a heavy finger on the shutter release, returns to the original position, creating a very lightly separated double-image. In subject motion blur, a major distinction is between the way a light subject moves against a dark background, and vice versa. Time and direction also matter.

FAMILIARIZE YOURSELF WITH YOUR LENSES' PERFORMANCE

How sharp should the focused area be? Not an easy question to answer when you are looking at a single image at 100% magnification on the computer screen. And as we know, lenses were not created equal in this respect. If you have an SLR with several lenses, some of them will perform better than others — under ideal conditions. A simple and worthwhile preparation is to find a subject to which you can always return easily, such as a fixture at home, and photograph it at the same scale with different lenses. This glass and iron sculpture is my choice. It should have a good, sharply contrasting edge at the centre, as this does. There are some obvious differences between these four lenses. Having test shots like this on file helps when you are deciding on the sharpness of a real photograph.

Nikon 18-200mm at 62mm   Nikon 18-200mm at 112mm   Zeiss Planar 85mm   Micro-Nikkor 105mm

DEFAULT BLUR IS GAUSSIAN

Most focus blur is not only radial but its effect on the image follows a Gaussian distribution. This means, in effect, that the blurred image of a point source of light fades away from the center like the 2D projection of a 3D Gaussian bell-shaped curve, as shown here. You can see this in action in Photoshop by creating a white dot on a black background and then applying Gaussian blur: Filter > Blur > Gaussian Blur (to see the effect clearly, give the dot a radius of at least a few pixels).

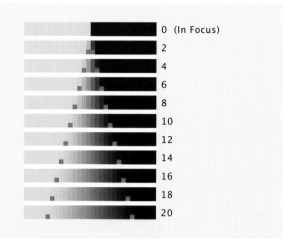

0 (In Focus)
2
4
6
8
10
12
14
16
18
20

f1.4

f1.4

f6.3

f6.3

f16

f16

Defocussing a point source

A specular reflection in a convex surface, such as this lacquer bowl and silver containers, is probably the ideal feature in a photograph for displaying the effect of focus blur. In these example sequences of details from the same image, the first row shows progressive blurring from sharp as the lens at full aperture f1.4 is progressively focused forward (closer to the camera), the second row shows the same focus settings at the smaller aperture of f6.3, and the third row is at the much smaller aperture of f16. Note that the classic radial blurring of point sources is really only obvious at a wide aperture; the blurred points at smaller apertures retain more of their original shape.

IDENTIFYING BLUR FOR REPAIR

GALLERY OF BLUR TYPES

Uni-directional camera shake
Specular highlights in the metal surface are good indicators of the direction, uniformity, and length of motion blur. As it affects the entire image, this is clearly camera shake. Extremely straight blur movements like this are also typical of motion blur caused by slippage or knocks to a camera mounted on a tripod.

Before correction

Basic focus blur
The problem here, as revealed by a magnified view, is an overall softening of focus, typical of focus blur. An analysis of this with Focus Magic shows a blur width of 6 pixels.

After correction

Original

After Noise Ninja repair

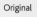

13 Pixels

Slight multi-directional camera shake

A magnified view of the selected area shows a consistent pattern that reveals a 13-pixel shift— just within the limits to expect repair—but with a curve at one end like a hook, which will limit the effectiveness of repair tools.

Pronounced multi-directional camera shake

The camera shake here is deliberate and long—and moved around the subject—but it also combines with subject motion blur. Analyzing two areas of the image show the curved movement of the bulls' horns—specific and different from other movements such as the matador's—but the area of the ground upper left show the actual camera movement, a curve towards the lower right, with a jerk at the end.

IDENTIFYING BLUR FOR REPAIR

GALLERY OF BLUR TYPES (CONTINUED)

Pronounced unidirectional camera shake
A magnified view of the man's head (and we can see that he appears to be standing still) shows at least two clear points of movement, in the same direction, of some 40 pixels, which is too great to attempt any repair.

PROGRESSIVE FOCUS BLUR

In most images of scenes with some depth to them, you can expect a progressive increase in focus blur. In this scene, inside a Burmese temple, magnified views of three sections show a visual defocussing in the direction of the arrow. Using Focus Magic to make an analysis of the amount of blur by clicking the Detect button confirms the progression.

Simple, short subject motion blur

A fishing trawler entering harbor has a predictable and known movement in one direction, and at a slow shutter speed because of the light (pre-dawn), you would expect some short motion blur. The obvious places in the image to look are narrow edges perpendicular to the expected movement — the vertical rigging — and indeed they do reveal blurring, in contrast to the horizontal rigging, which doesn't.

Complex subject motion blur

The standing figure moves predictably from right to left, by approximately 5% of the image frame, equivalent to about 200 pixels. However, different parts, such as the arms, can be expected to move in different directions and by different amounts.

REPAIRING FOCUS BLUR

In principle, sharpening can be put into three categories (though the practice may be different). The first is sharpening to overcome softness introduced during capture, of which there are two components: optical softness from the lens, and digital softness from the sensor. Most lenses show soft spots in different parts of the images area and at different apertures. The sensor and the processing of the signal it captures also introduces softness when continuous tones are translated into pixels on a regular sampling grid, and details that are finer than the sampling frequency are averaged by interpolation. The second category is sharpening for creative or repair reasons, applied to details identified by the photographer. The third is sharpening targeted to the needs of the output device, such as a printer. Although capture-repair-output is a logical time sequence for performing sharpening, standard professional practice in photography tends to demand that images stay unsharpened until final use. Stock agencies in particular, and a few clients, are familiar with sharpening artifacts, and may well reject images that have been sharpened in such an obvious way.

This, however, is a contentious area, because the real reason for not wanting sharpening performed early in the workflow is the danger of artifacting. The key artifacts in question, which are always sufficient for a stock agency, for example, to reject the image, are scattered dark pixels and halos, both bordering edges. Acceptable, and usually not even visible, on a printed page, these are usually obvious and objectionable in an image viewed on-screen. The reason they appear at all is that throughout photography

Some, but only a few, blurred images can be restored, using some form of sharpening. It's important to distinguish between this and normal digital sharpening procedures.

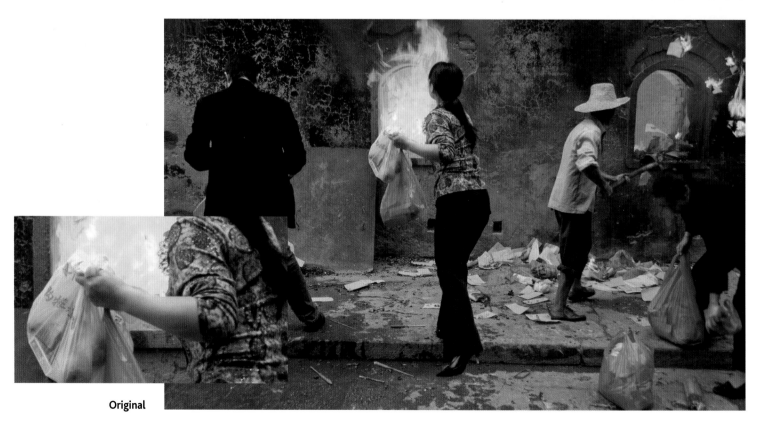

Original

and printing, the usual way of sharpening an image is to increase the contrast at edges within the image. This has everything to do with the psychology of perception, because we judge sharpness most in local detail and in particular in terms of contrast.

In practice, the first two purposes are usually combined, and can usefully be kept separate from the third. Sharpening is destructive, and procedural sharpening passes are always best left until the last minute, and on a copy, because the amount of sharpening is partly determined by final use—the size of reproduction and the characteristics of the output device. This leaves creative/repair sharpening, which is much less amenable to procedural techniques, as we'll now see. It also needs to be done circumspectly, paying special attention to avoiding tell-tale artifacts as evidence, for the commercial reasons just mentioned.

First, procedural repair. This means an imaging operation, such as a filter, applied algorithmically, usually across the entire image. The opposite is direct

PHOTOSHOP SMART SHARPEN

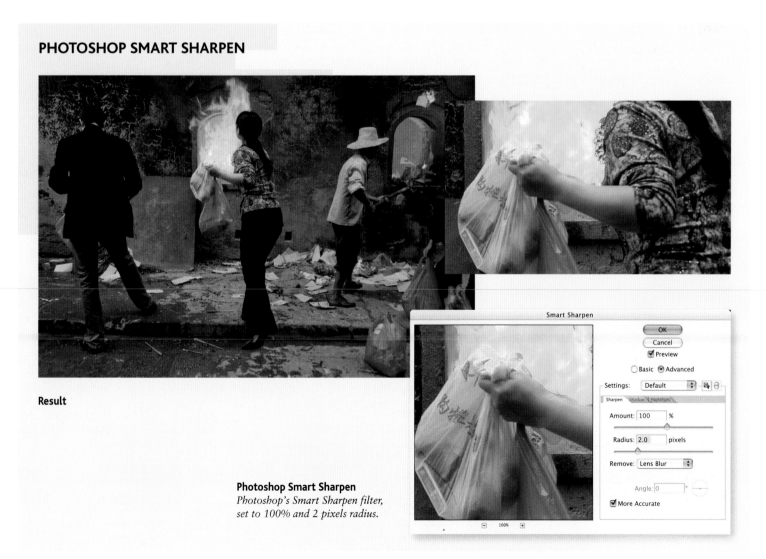

Result

Photoshop Smart Sharpen
Photoshop's Smart Sharpen filter, set to 100% and 2 pixels radius.

REPAIRING FOCUS BLUR

brushwork. There are two schools of thought here. The argument in favor of procedural sharpening is that if the cause of the blurring had an overall effect and can be analyzed, it can be reversed with an algorithm. The major argument against is that sharpness is perceptual and so largely a matter of individual judgment, so sharpening the entire image is overkill. The argument in favor of brushwork applied to chosen details is that this can address just the areas that you decide are important, and do so without pixellated artifacts. Against this is the ethical point that brushwork verges on alteration and manipulation.

A better procedural choice is dedicated deblurring software, of which there is surprisingly little available commercially. I say surprising because deblurring and image restoration receives a great deal of scientific attention, and is used in military applications. One program available on both Windows and Mac platforms is shown here, Focus Magic. It works on both focus blur and motion blur. In the former, the blur is radial outwards, and the software attempts to reverse this process by moving pixel edges back towards the center of what it computes to be the original source. In the case of motion blur, the process is in principle the same,

DXO'S LENS SOFTNESS DECONVOLUTION

DxO Optics Pro
This tool allows you to see a before and after view as you work.

As one part of its overall image processing, DxO uses a painstaking analysis of specific lens-sensor combinations to calculate their exact blurring effect in each part of the frame and at every aperture setting. The algorithm reverses this blurring, with the default auto setting being the software engineer's judgment. A slider allows the user to lessen or increase the strength. Because this deblurring is applied to known defects in the lens and sensor, it differs from ordinary USM sharpening in that it is applied selectively.

DxO Optics Pro
The default settings in Lens Softness using DxO Optics Pro. This applies pre-calculated corrections to a lens and camera combination that has already been analyzed and is in the software database.

but the pixels are shifted in one direction only. As explained in the box "Convolution and deconvolution," deblurring is based on analysis of the original capture. Focus Magic does this by having the user examine the blur shape and put numbers to it. DxO Optics Pro, as part of its Raw conversion package, refers to lens modules that the company has already prepared by analyzing the performance of individual lenses used with particular sensors.

There are limits to what deblurring software can do, and it works best when there are plenty of linear boundaries to work on. The practical limits are effectively less than 20 pixels, meaning less than 20 pixels blur width in the case of focus blur and smear length in the case of motion blur. There are technical constraints also, as processing time increases exponentially with the pixel distance, but as the developer, Eric Schwerzel, explains, if the blur distance is more than 20 pixels, the image is so flawed that you might as well downsize the file because it will reproduce in print or on-screen satisfactorily only if small.

Returning to Photoshop and other image-editing programs, most have similar filters, and there are procedural alternatives to USM (Unsharp Mask). Smart Sharpen in the latest version of Photoshop (CS3) allows you to select sharpening aimed at optical blur via the Remove drop-down menu. Lens Blur deals with focus blur, and Motion Blur does as it says, requiring the user to set the angle. Another effective treatment, with little noise effect and reasonable control over halos, is High Pass sharpening. This is a two-step layered procedure, in which a duplicate layer is made of the image. A high pass filter (*Filter > Other > High Pass*) is then applied to the duplicate layer, then this is changed to Hard Light mode. Overlay mode is slightly less strong in its effect, and Soft Light less strong again. The High Pass filter retains edge details where maximum color transitions occur. However, it must be said that at this time the Photoshop deblurring filters are not at all sophisticated in their operation, and fall short of the dedicated third-party software just described.

FOCUS MAGIC'S DEDICATED DEBLURRING

This software works by first calculating the blur radius in pixels, and then applying a special algorithm designed to reverse the process that created the blur. The recommended procedure is for the user to examine the image at high magnification, for example 300%, find point sources, and measure the radius of the blur disc. The software will also make its own estimation when you click on a part of the image. Some trial and error experiments at different radius settings are useful in judging the most effective one. The strength setting defaults at 100%, but this is, as is usual in software, the engineer's estimate, and the user can reduce or increase. My own feelings are that 100% is a little too aggressive, with a greater risk of halos than 75% or even 50%.

Focus Magic
Also aimed at the lettering on the plastic bag, Focus Magic first detects and estimates the amount of deconvolution required — here 2 pixels.

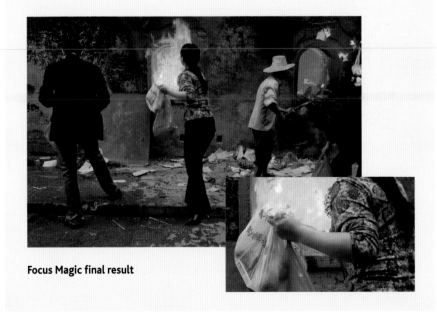

Focus Magic final result

REPAIRING FOCUS BLUR

CONVOLUTION AND DECONVOLUTION

Processing optical blur and lens softness is not a simple procedure, as it means first identifying the amount and type of blur and then attempting to reverse the process mathematically. Lens blur is described mathematically by convolution, repairing it is deconvolution. Convolution is a mathematical operator that combines two functions to make a third, and one example in optics is a shadow, which is the convolution of two things—the shape of the light source and the object that casts the shadow. Optical blur is the convolution of the sharp image with the shape of the aperture diaphragm in the lens. In other words, apply the aperture shape at a particular f-stop in a certain way to a point in the image, and the result will be a specific shape and size of blur. Motion blur is also a convolution, of the sharp image and a linear movement.

In the example here, convolution can be thought of as a moving average applied to each pixel over a certain radius. At its simplest, a black pixel on a white background is averaged to a pale gray. A solid color, say all black or all white, is unchanged. Applying this across the entire image, pixel by pixel, has the effect of blurring sharp points and edges but leaving solid areas untouched. This is the blurring process.

The aim of deconvolution is to reverse what happened, and so de-blur the image. It depends very much on being able to describe the original blurring precisely. The PSF (point spread function) describes this mathematically, but is difficult to calculate unless the software designer knows the exact performance of the lens in combination with the sensor. The shape of the blur from a single point can vary considerably from the simplest case of a round disc, depending on the characteristics of the lens and sensor, its position in the image frame, the f-stop, and so on.

Deconvolution (or deblurring) effectively sharpens the image, and the difference between this and normal sharpening is largely a matter of terminology. In a sense, deconvolution/deblurring is a form of sharpening with a specific goal, while normal sharpening is open-ended.

…but black blurs to black…

…and white blurs to white.

In focus blurring, a black pixel on a white background would be convolved to grey…

Non-procedural restoration works in an entirely different way, and is more intuitive and hands-on. There are few "silver bullet" solutions here that will magically and quickly improve the image, instead there is painstaking brushwork at 100% and 200%, calling on the skills of the miniaturist rather than the computer engineer. The key steps can be summarized as follows: identify where in the image the eye will travel to most insistently to search for detail, then work on these at a high magnification to enhance local contrast and edges, working with a variety of brushes. Which brushes is a matter of personal preference, as is the choice of brush hardness, but the Clone Stamp and Smudge tools are both useful, not least because they make use of existing pixels and pixel distribution.

The examples here tell the story best, as this kind of retouching does not lend itself to generalization.

Brushwork can, of course, be combined with procedural sharpening, either to make very detailed selections before applying a filter, or to take over in key details when the filter has done as much as is realistically possible.

A four-way comparison
Clockwise from top left: no correction, DxO, Focus Magic, and Photoshop. The most successful in this example is Focus Magic, with no unnecessary edge-sharpening with consequent halos (as happens with Photoshop, the least successful). DxO also handles the lettering well, but is less successful than Focus Magic with the lace outlined against the flames.

No correction

DxO

Photoshop

Focus magic

REPAIR TO EXTEND FOCUS

The software techniques developed to repair soft focus can be applied effectively, though with considerable effort, to extend the apparent depth of field in a photograph.

Although an image that is completely out of focus and nowhere sharp is usually considered a reject (though not always), gradations of sharpness are an absolutely normal part of photography. Because of the way the eye and brain work, we are only rarely ever conscious of this kind of optical blur in real life, as our gaze flicks rapidly from one part of a scene to another, refocusing almost instantaneously. Nevertheless, more than a century of looking at photographs has made depth of field (see definition) a normal feature of imagery. Particularly in a long-focus picture, it is completely acceptable to have blur at the front and back around a limited sharp zone, and even attractive.

Because lowlight shooting hand held inevitably means a wide aperture, almost all images shot with a long focal length will have very shallow depth of field. Obviously, one of the shooting strategies is to use this creatively, making compositions that work around a single sharp point, perhaps using the blurred zones to point this out or else as a color wash. At other times, we would really have preferred to have greater depth of field but have to settle for shallow.

For some distance beyond the depth of field, the soft focus can in principle be treated in the same way as we've just seen with overall soft-focus blur. If it's possible to isolate these zones somehow, they can be processed with a filter such as that from Focus Magic. Dividing an image according to depth is at best a fairly arbitrary procedure. By doing it after the event, there is no direct measurement possible to construct a depth map (sometimes known as a z map after the 3D axis that defines depth). The only evidence is a commonsense reconstruction from what you can see in the image, but in a case like the example here, there are no ambiguities. We know what a truck looks like, and which parts will be in front of which others. Remember also that here we're after visual effect, not precise measurement. The color-coded focus plan is included to show approximately the plan for extending the depth of field. It is not for any procedural use, just a quick analysis of the different planes of softness.

The principle is to first to decide how much of the soft zones beyond the depth of field can realistically be brought back towards sharpness. Bearing in mind the 20-pixel maximum practical radius (see page 122) and the fact that large-radius filtering runs the risk of looking unnatural, it may be worth selecting two or three zones of increasing blur, then running the filter at different settings for each.

There are several options for doing this, but all depend on some form of manual brushing. One is to paint a mask on the image to cover a zone (Quick Mask in Photoshop), then applying the filter to that, repeating the process for other zones. Another, which allows a better overall view, is to apply the filter at a particular setting to an underlying duplicate layer, and then selectively erase the top layer. A third method is simply to apply the filter, then use the History Brush to restore the already-sharply-focused areas to their original state.

DEPTH OF FIELD

This is the extent in front of and behind a sharply focused distance that still appear to the eye to be acceptably sharp. It depends on aperture, focal length, and the distance between camera and subject, but above all is a subjective impression. The smaller the aperture, the shorter the focal length, and the further the scene from the camera, the greater the depth of field. Nevertheless, what one person deems acceptably sharp may not be the same as judged by someone else.

focus blur analysis
Comparing different parts of the truck shows the progression of focus blurring towards the back.

Focus plan
For the purposes of this demonstration, the image is divided into focus zones, each needing different amounts of correction.

Motion blur analysis
The first step is to see if there is any motion blur in addition to the focus blur. At high magnification, the sharpest point on the truck — the number on the tank — does indeed show unequal edge sharpness. The curve on the figure 7 is instructive; the sharpest section of the edge is at about 40°.

Focus Magic preview and correction
Each zone is selected by painting in Quick Mask, and specific correction applied. This is zone 4 on the plan.

Focus Magic correction
Focus Magic applied as motion blur correction to 10 pixels.

The final result

The original image of a truck on a Canadian highway was shot from an overpass with an extremely long and fast telephoto lens. With a focal length of 600 mm and at f4, the depth of field was extremely shallow.

REPAIRING MOTION BLUR

Going back to the types of blur identified on pages 96-103, the key difference between focus blur and motion blur from the point of view of repairing them is not how they were caused but rather the shape of the blur. The Point Spread Function for focus blur gives a radial pattern—from point to disc, in other words—but motion blur is unidirectional and at a particular angle.

Although the causes are quite different, from the viewpoint of image analysis and repair, motion blur is like focus blur but in one direction only, and can be treated in a similar way.

You could say that both focus and motion blur are versions of the same effect, and for repairing them the software problems are similar.

The procedure, too, is similar. First the motion blur has to be calculated, in terms of how many pixels in length and in what direction, measured as an angle. Then the software has to attempt to move edge-defining pixels back to where they should have been, by exactly that many pixels and in that direction. This is no easy calculation, because it is applied to the entire image and within this the algorithm must distinguish between edges and more amorphous zones. Photoshop has such a filter, which can be found by choosing *Filter > Sharpen > Smart Sharpen* and, under the Remove heading, selecting Motion Blur. However, as the example here shows, this is really just a variant on unsharp masking, and while it may improve the appearance to an extent (depending on the specific image), it is not actually reversing the motion blur.

The more effective software is Focus Magic which, up to a blur distance of several pixels, can impressively reveal detail that was not visible in the original image. An acid test of the efficiency of motion blur repair is what the software does to a distinct, simple line that is more or less perpendicular to the blur angle. Typically, it appears in the original as a thicker band instead of a line. Effective repair will restore it to a line.

Nun

Small details that contain lines or edges running in different directions are ideal for assessing direction and amount. Here, the fold in the cloth is sharper than the edge. Matching the direction of the fold by eye with the Blur Direction setting confirms the direction at 100°.

HAND HELD

Before

After

Before

Having established the blur direction, using the plentiful detail in the bead jewelry, experiment with different Blur Distances. Here two pixels is too little, and six pixels too much. The ideal setting is four pixels. See the effect on the eyes and on the white beads.

Too much

Too little

Just right

After

Detail view

As ever, the best way to see your work is to view it at 100% or a multiple thereof (200%, 300%, 400%, and so on). These scales do not require interpolation to be displayed, so are the most accurate.

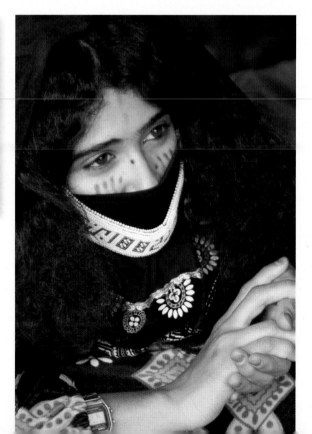

DETECTING MOVEMENT

Here the useful detail is part of the rim of the man's glasses, showing a typical double edge. The lower ends of the highlighted edges indicate the direction of the movement.

Focus Magic
For this image a strong 75% Amount was applied to a dramatic 16 pixel Blur Distance.

Before

After

PREDICTABLE SHAPES

The key to this kind of correction is finding the most appropriate detail in the image.
Circles and other predictable curves are good because they identify a progression.
This ring also contains specular highlights, making it even easier to measure the blur.
For confirmation, look at a similar frame that is sharply focused.

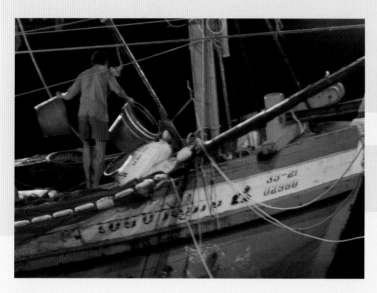

Before

Focus Magic
*Correcting the image using Focus Magic
I applied a Blur Width setting of 6.*

After

REPAIRING COMBINED BLUR TYPES

So far, we've looked at focus blur and motion blur as if they were isolated entities. They do indeed have different causes, but in reality, working in low light means wide open on the aperture at the same time as a relatively slow shutter speed. Both types of blur are often combined, in which case it takes close examination and a sort of diagnostic experience to discover this. Going back to pages 96-103, motion blur is actually the easier to identify with certainty, at least if it spreads over several rather than few pixels, simply for the reason that it has a consistent trajectory. A point source or a corner are ideal if they exist in the photograph, and can be confirmed by looking at other similar details in other parts of the image. If the angle is the same, the diagnosis is motion blur. Focus blur is more difficult to isolate, because this kind of softness is already an integral part of digital capture—the general softening effect of the sensor recording the image, combined with the always inevitable lens defects (there is no perfect lens).

The repair problem is compounded when there is both focus and motion blur in the same image, but this is relatively common in lowlight photography and should be expected.

Knowing this, it makes sense to try and identify first—to isolate, in effect—any component of motion blur, simply because it is the most identifiable. Look for a consistent shift in the same angular direction all across the image. It's essential to identify the angle, because the next step is to look for softness perpendicular to this—at 90°. If there is a blurring in this direction, it means that there is also focus blur at work.

The repair procedure follows the diagnostics. First reduce or eliminate the motion blur, using the techniques already described. What remains will be the focus blur, which needs a second pass of this flavor of filter. Each pass of the filter introduces some risk of image damage, particularly at high strengths, so that there are even more limits than usual on how much you can expect to repair the image. Nevertheless, as the examples here shows, it can work. As with every other kind of repair that depends on sharpening (of some kind), it works best to a small degree. Repair is always a delicate procedure.

Original

Returning the to the photograph of the Burmese Buddha statue, we can see that under close inspection there is both focus blur and motion blur, the latter to a small amount.

Motion Blur first attempt

The mouth and nose reveal some double-edging that suggests motion blur. Using Focus Magic and experimenting with direction and distance gives 20° and 14 pixels. An amount of 75% will give a significant improvement.

Motion Blur second attempt

100% gives even more correction, and no apparent over-sharpening.

Focus Blur detection

This done, we now use Focus Magic to help detect the amount of focus blur, concentrating on the eye as the natural focus for any viewer looking at the image. The blur width is 5 pixels, and a moderate 50% correction amount gives an improvement without over-sharpening.

Finished

The final result, with two passes of blur correction, motion and focus.

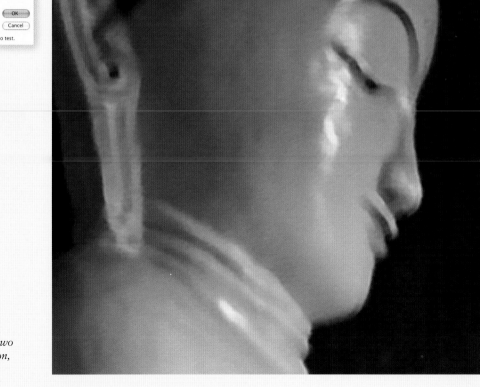

GROSS MOTION BLUR

. . . .

In the example here, the motion blur is so strong that it is an inextricable part of the image. In fact, it is due to a slow shutter speed and a panning action, The immediate issue is whether or not the photograph makes it at all. Does it succeed, or rather could it succeed with poet-production help? At this degree of motion blur, there are no generalizations. Everything is in the specific. Opinion also tends to be specific, and personal. Let's say that in this case (a mistake, actually, as I had the shutter speed set slower than I had thought) I had intended the picture to be sharp and was disappointed that I had got it wrong, but that later I grew to like it. The problem, again always specific, was that there was no anchor point of real sharpness anywhere in the frame. In particular, the eyes at least needed to be sharp to some degree. In general, the eyes are the focus of any face being looked at, and it's almost impossible to escape the need for them to have sharp edges.

Major shifts that are obvious at a glance when looking at a small version of a photograph are an entirely different issue, in which the blur is a part of the image's appeal and any repair is directed towards this.

Using the techniques already described, the motion blur here can be analyzed to a distance of many more pixels than the capability of focus repair software. Also, at this amount of movement, the smearing is wobbly, which lends itself even less well to procedural treatment. The only reasonable procedure is manual, in other words brushing by hand.

The interesting point here is that very few parts of the image need to be sharp in order to make it visually acceptable. What rules is a knowledge of human perception. The content, even though unfamiliar to most Westerners, is nevertheless quite understandable. A Vietnamese man wearing a military pith helmet of the Vietnam War vintage, is smoking a large bamboo pipe. This reads at a glance. All that is needed technically is to introduce some key sharpness at a few well-chosen points, after which the remaining blur will be completely acceptable. The details that need sharpening are precisely located but obvious, and can be summarized as follows: the eyes as always, a re-definition of the mouth, and nearby distinct edges. No more than that. The unusual pipe does not need to be treated because a viewer's eyes will always be drawn to the man's face, and it is in any case fairly obvious as it is.

The handwork is a kind of painting, and the main tools are the smudge tool, which pushes pixels and so has the ability to harden up an edge, and the clone stamp tool, which here can take a small sharp part of an edge and extend it into zones where the edges have become blurred. At this shutter speed, half a second, both camera shake/panning and subject movement have contributed to the motion blur.

Before

After

USING THE BUCKLE

Spotting the blur
The metalwork on the pith helmet is an ideal indicator of the direction of the motion blur.

Focus Magic improvement
The maximum setting in Focus Magic makes a distinct improvement.

Negative effect
However, this blur correction applied to the entire image creates unacceptable artifacting in the more delicate areas of the face.

Areas for manual correction
Instead, the key zones for manual retouching are identified as the eyes, ear and nose.

Nose plan
The plan of attack for the eye, using the Smudge tool in specific directions, followed by a darkening with the Burn tool.

Ear plan
The clone tool settings chosen for sharpening the edges of the nose and mouth, working from the outside for the nose and from the inside for the lip.

Eye result
The result of the eye retouching.

Nose result
The result for the nose and mouth.

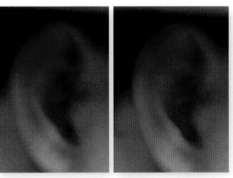

Ear result
The result for the ear.

FRAME SELECTION AND LAYER BLENDING

Shooting extra frames to guarantee sharpness is good practice when the lighting conditions are pushing the limits on camera shake, motion blur and accurate focusing (see pages 72-77). What then usually happens is that the sequence is examined carefully and at magnification to find the best shot, technically and creatively. The choice may be obvious, but sometimes you may find that two or three frames each have some advantage. The focus may be sharper in one but the composition better in another, or there may be some unwanted subject motion blur in the sharpest version. In this case, there is another solution, though it may not appeal to everyone. This involves taking the best of one and adding to to another.

In a series of similarly composed frames, there may be differences in sharpness and blur that can be exploited by combining the best of each in a layered composite.

The principle is straightforward—layering the images in register, then erasing the unwanted parts of one. As long as the frames are matched for their content, color, brightness and contrast, this gives you the freedom to have the best of both (or of several). There are ethical considerations because this is a form of manipulation, and not too many steps away from the kind of fictional image in which subjects are added from one to another, but under certain circumstances, particularly when nothing much is changing in the scene in front of you, it may be justified.

Under the circumstances illustrated here, where we are essentially dealing with a rapid burst of shooting, matching color, brightness and contrast is not normally an issue. Typically, load the frames together into the Raw converter (you'll notice that I'm assuming throughout this book that everything is shot in Raw), Select All and adjust as necessary. Even if there were exposure differences between frames, simply toggle back and forth from one frame to another and adjust until they are visually matched. More demanding is getting the frames in register. The manual method is tedious: copy one frame onto another as a separate layer, set the Opacity of the upper layer to somewhere around 60% so that you can see both images but one is more prominent, zoom in to 50% or 100%, and use the arrow keys to align them as well as possible. When they seem to be in register, set the Opacity of the upper layer back to 100% and check the register by toggling the visibility of the upper layer off and on repeatedly. Registration becomes more difficult if there has been rotation between the images, because to adjust this (in *Edit > Transform > Rotate*) you need to see the entire image, making exact alignment harder to judge.

This operation has been made much more feasible in Photoshop CS3 with the Auto-Align Layers function. First lock the layer you want to use as a reference (if it is the Background image it will automatically be locked), then select both or all of the layers that you want to align, including the reference layer, then go to *Edit > Auto-Align Layers*. The Reposition Only option should normally be sufficient if there was little camera movement between frames, but the Auto option will automatically make whatever geometric transformations are needed. Note that because this automatic alignment is based on the software's analysis of content, it may make compromises that you don't like. For example, if there has been a parallax shift of foreground details due to slight movement in the camera position, the alignment process, which is of course based on image content, may base its calculation on foreground or background. In the example of the bird in the cage (see box, page 123), the Auto option attempts a distortion fit, but fails to correct some of the horizontal bars, as indicated in the lower image.

Finish the alignment if necessary by using any of the tools in *Edit > Free Transform*, and/or making tonal adjustments to even out any exposure or color differences. Once the images are aligned and matched for tone and color, use the Eraser for a direct replacement of less-sharp areas. An alternative to the Eraser is to mask the layers which is completely non-destructive, but the undo tool is always available in ordinary editing and is quicker and easier to access, and creates smaller files.

HAND HELD

NIGHT-TIME TRAFFIC AND PEOPLE

While these adjustments are not absolutely critical in this case, this sequence of three shots (taken within the period of a single minute) allows a final composite that both eliminates the streaking of moving vehicles and a shows denser mass of pedestrians. The workflow goes as follows: first compare the images and work out a plan of what to keep and what to eliminate, then cut and paste them into a layer stack, align them and finally erase the unwanted elements.

Choosing the images
Examining the three images side by side, I could quickly devise a plan. The center frame is the reference image, in which most of the traffic is stationary, bar three moving vehicles. The left frame has much the same traffic and can be used to replace the vehicle streaks. The right-hand frame has generally more crowded sidewalks, and the building on the right has a more easily readable blue-tinted video screen.

Auto-Align
Begin the Auto-align process by clicking File > Automate > Photomerge *and selecting Auto.*

Photoshop Layers
The three images are added to the same image as layers.

Erasing
Using the Erase tool or, if you are familiar with it the Masking options, parts of the upper layer are removed to reveal the similar image from below. Here, for example, the blurred van is removed.

Raw processing
All the images are processed at once in ACR.

FRAME SELECTION AND LAYER BLENDING

COMBINING BEST GESTURE AND SHAKE-FREE BACKGROUND

From a sequence of nearly identical frames, all shot at 1/15 second with an optically stabilized lens, there were a few shake-free and also a choice of the position and actions of the priest, who was cleaning the altar of this large and busy temple in southern China. Combining the sharpest frame, free of camera shake, with the preferred gesture of the man allowed the best of both worlds.

RAW conversion
Both of these images were processed identically, here using DxO Optics Pro for the Raw conversion.

Lightbox
The choice was narrowed down to two, which were examined in iView MediaPro's Lightbox mode. The image on the left is the shake-free version, on the right the preferred composition.

First choice of subject
The preferred priest image.

Auto-Align
Using the Auto-align function in Photoshop, the two images are registered. As the two separate layers show, there is an offset.

First choice background
The preferred background.

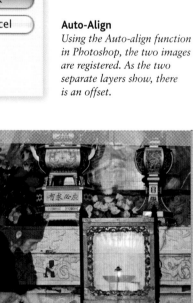

Temporary opacity
In order to erase only those areas with underlying matched background, the upper layer is set to 50%.

Straightening

With both layers selected, the combined image is rotated (Edit > Transform > Rotate) to straighten up horizontals and verticals.

Erasing upper layer

The upper layer is erased selectively, here made obvious by making the lower layer invisible for the purposes of demonstration. Note that because the two pictures were not framed identically, the very top is left untouched, although it has some camera shake, this is judged to be unimportant because it is away from the picture's center of interest.

Final result

The layers are finally collapsed and the image cropped for the final combined result.

SPOTTING MOVEMENT

Shot 1

This is the first of two shots of a domestic bird, which is always restless on its perch. While that is still a limited range of movement, there is still a surprising variety, as we'll see.

Shot 2

In the moments between frames, the bird has managed to turn its head to look in a different direction, moved its tail to balance itself and apparently lean away from the camera.

Identified motion

To clarify the motion the two images above are overlaid here. The arrows indicate the shift, and therefore the direction which needs compensating for.

TRACKING FOR SHARPNESS

As anyone who has had the experience of aiming at a target knows, whether with a rifle or in archery, holding steady on a fixed target is by no means easy, both mechanically and psychologically. Indeed, the longer you try and hold, the more likely involuntary movements are (first discussed on pages 76-77).

Because it is easier to hold a camera steady and on target when moving it smoothly than when stationary, panning and other forms of tracking are worthwhile techniques for keeping the subject sharp.

Introduce movement, however, and things become more fluid and steady, due to inertia. The same applies to handheld photography, and the time honored technique of panning, by swinging the camera from one side to another to follow a moving subject, can produce surprisingly sharp results at slow shutter speeds. The principle is that you make use of inertia (mass × velocity) to overwhelm smaller jiggles. When combined with vibration reduction technology in the lens (see pages 82-85), this can be a surprisingly effective technique in keeping at least some part of the image sharp.

Panning is the action of moving the camera to hold steady on a moving subject, but the reverse situation is also possible—moving the camera from a moving vehicle to hold onto a stationary subject. The detail effects are different, but the principle is the same. There is always an amount of uncertainty in doing this, but it is quite often worth trying, just to see what turns out. The instant feedback from digital lets you judge immediately whether to save or delete, and whether to continue with different settings.

There are some perceptual factors at work, too. Just as the range between sharp and blurred focus is greater with a fast lens used to isolate a detail at full aperture to help the focused subject to stand out, so the motion smearing from a panning shot helps to accentuate the part of the subject held in crisp detail.

Increasing the time that the shutter is open, and particularly over half a second, makes the outcome quite uncertain, not only because of prolonged subject movement, but camera shake makes a bigger contribution. The effect then merges with the subject of the following pages, intentional motion blur.

Migrating beast
*White-eared Kob beginning
their annual migration across
the Nile valley in southern
Sudan, photographed with a
180mm lens from a height of
about 100 feet, through the
open door of a light aircraft.
With the aircraft travelling at
around 100mph, the antelope
running at around 30mph,
and a reverse pan with the
camera (against the direction
of movement), this is a
complicated tracking shot
that manages to hold most of
the animals sharp at a shutter
speed of 1/35 sec, wide open
at f2.8.*

FAR LEFT **Highland stag**
*Using a 400mm lens from a
standing position, a Scottish
Highland stag captured at
1/60sec and ISO 400.*

LEFT **Tracking vehicles**
*A different kind of tracking,
also from a moving vehicle,
in this case a boat in the
Gulf of Thailand at dusk.
The shutter speed of 1/3 sec
with a focal length of
200mm is far too long
for a truly sharp hand-held
shot, even with vibration
reduction activated, but the
combined motion of the two
boats, plus the steadying
effect of a slow pan, give an
interesting result that achieves
just-acceptable sharpness of
the man at the tiller.*

MAKING MOTION BLUR WORK

Revealing motion
A Sufi adherent in Omdurman, Sudan, performs an ecstatic whirling dance. Fading daylight gave the choice of a sharp image at a high ISO, or the much more evocative and dynamic result chosen here by using a shutter speed of 1/30sec.

Motion blur is not all bad. Despite all the efforts that we normally make to avoid it and correct it, which we've just examined in more than usual depth, there are occasions when it can actually make the image. Most photography has some documentary quality to it in the sense that it is showing a lucid view of something—a place, an event, a person—but photographs also have graphic qualities just as do paintings. The streaking and smearing effect of significant blur reduces the information content, but it can make the image more interesting, even intriguing. Sometimes photographs work better if they don't reveal their content all at once.

In particular, motion blur does best what it's name suggests. It gets across the sense of movement, and it does so in a graphically dynamic way. Moving objects photographed with a shutter speed sufficiently short to freeze them against their background have a curiously static quality at odds with the event. There may not even be any clues in the picture to show that a car or a train, for instance, was actually in motion. It could have been parked or stopped, and even if we know that it was moving in real life (a car in the fast lane of a highway is unlikely to be stationary), the quality of speed is often missing in the photograph. This does not necessarily matter at all, as we're accustomed to the way photographs look, but it does open the opportunity for using a relatively slow shutter speed to enhance the sensation of speed.

The key to all of this is occasional use. Using motion blur frequently as a graphic device simply becomes a mannerism, and it is much more effective when it appears as a surprise. Shooting hand held means introducing movement in to the image by the way you move the camera—controlled and prolonged camera shake, if you like. This adds to any movement in the subject for an effect that can be complex and difficult to predict, which is one of its attractions. There are a number of examples from the history of photography, and one of the most notable were the several "motion" series shot by Ernst Haas in the 1950s, on subjects as diverse as bullfighting, rodeos, and motor racing. The swirling and streaked smears of color give an impressionistic effect. The results are always specific to the situation, so this technique calls for experimentation. Two key variables are the shutter speed and the kind of movement you introduce by shifting, shaking, jerking, or rotating the camera.

Quite apart from the various shooting and software techniques to control, minimize and avoid motion blur, it lends itself to deliberate use in creating graphic, impressionist images.

Very long shutter

Panning with a long lens (400mm efl) and a very slow speed, the aim of this shot was to convey, just, the top-hatted attire of brokers in a City of London street—a deliberately impressionistic treatment that was felt to be stronger than a literal and sharp image.

Getting nowhere fast

ABOVE *A planned shot of a hotel gym, where a slow speed of 1/4 sec at f9 was needed in order to give some sense of action to what otherwise could have been a lifeless image.*

On scene

LEFT *As part of a feature on traffic accidents in Bangkok, this overturned pick-up, its driver already taken to hospital, was photographed with a deliberate jerkiness and at 1/3 sec (at ISO 800) for a sense of movement.*

RAW FOR LOW LIGHT

The wide ranges of color temperature and tonal distribution in lowlight shooting makes the Raw format even more useful than usual.

Using the Raw format for shooting is now the professional standard in almost all kinds of photography (news, sports, and when fast delivery overrides post-production are the notable exceptions to this rule). Its two most outstanding benefits are first that it preserves the capture data separate from whatever settings were applied at the time of shooting, so allowing color temperature, for example, to be chosen later. Second, it can record a wider dynamic range than other formats.

Given the typically major shifts of color from one scene to another in lowlight photography, and the fact that they are often unpredictable, the settings-change features alone make the Raw format almost essential. Most digital photographers are by now familiar with the concept of Raw, but to summarize briefly, these are proprietary image formats devised by the camera manufacturers, each one different, with the intention of receiving post-camera processing in specialist (often manufacturer specific) software tools. Saving images in Raw rather than going straight to JPEG or TIFF in-camera gives you access to the original capture data. All Raw converter software, and there are now many on the market, provides image editing tools to extract the maximum usable information from the data, and convert it to a useful format such as TIFF, JPEG, or DNG (the open-source Digital Negative format promoted by Adobe for archiving Raw files). Between the converters there are variations in the number of features, how the controls work, and the way they read and interpret the data (much of which is undocumented, being part of the camera manufacturers' code). Nevertheless, all do a good job.

High contrast is also a feature of many lowlight scenes that contain artificial lighting. This, as we saw on pages 48-57, is partly because of the pooling of light from localized sources (a result of the Inverse Square Law), and partly because the light sources themselves, such as desk lamps or street lights, appear in shot. High contrast scenes have a higher dynamic range than normal, and importantly, higher than can be rendered by a standard 8-bit image. Bit-depth is directly related to the dynamic range that a format can cover and, in the case of professional and serious amateur cameras, the sensor works in a higher bit-depth, typically 12-bits, but some at 10-bits and others at 14-bits. In other words, the sensor is capable of recording a greater range from highlights to shadows than most monitor screens and all printing devices can display, and at some point this has to be compressed or tone-mapped (see page 200). In non-Raw shooting, the camera's microprocessor does this, but a Raw converter and computer are a more powerful combination, have more sophisticated features, and above all, allow you to decide on the final result. For example, if highlights have been clipped, but not in all three color channels, a Raw converter can make a decent job of reconstructing the data from the surviving one or two channels. The same can be done with clipped shadows and, as happens with Photoshop's converter, for example, shadow detail can be opened up by the use of local operators that search neighboring pixels (for more on this, see pages 196-205).

As Raw converters develop and improve, they allow more and more of the normal workflow to be conducted within them. The raw converter in Photoshop CS3, for example, now contains cloning stamp and healing brush retouching tools. This makes for a more convenient, one-stop, way of working, so that under many circumstances you can make a final save directly from the Raw converter window without needing to open the image again and use other Photoshop tools. The major exception to this is noise reduction, unless you are happy to stay with the controls offered for this in the Raw converter. As we'll see on pages 146-155, there are important choices to be made in noise reduction, which might mean favoring a dedicated standalone program.

Adobe Camera Raw (ACR) defaults

For reference, this is the image as shot in Raw, opened as default in ACR with no changes. A large area is marked by the clipping warning (red pixels).

Restoring shadows

As the Recovery darkened the overall brightness of the image, Fill is increased to 50, which has the effect of restoring the shadows.

Recovery and fill

Of the various ways of approaching the translation from Raw to TIFF, this method focuses on maximum recovery of highlight clipping and an appropriate fill. The first step here, as the sun is obviously well overexposed, is to set Recovery to 100%, with the clipping warning (in red) visible.

Result

The combined Recovery and Fill changes have predictably lowered global contrast, so the Contrast slider is increased, creating this result.

RAW FOR LOW LIGHT

Automatic alternative
An alternative approach is to rely on Adobe Camera Raw's automated analysis of the image. This uses Recovery too, but much less than the previous example, and lowered Contrast.

Compensating
As the Exposure increase has worsened the highlight clipping, maximum Recovery is applied. The 100% Recovery has a spillover effect on mid-to-dark shadows, lowering them, and contributes to a general lowering of contrast. One way to deal with this would be through Brightness and Contrast sliders, but in this case I use the Curves tool.

Exposure adjustment
Yet another approach is to begin with the Exposure slider, taking advantage of the extra dynamic range from a 12-bit or 14-bit Raw file. Here, we use the previous Auto result as the starting point, increasing Exposure by one-and-a-half stops as a way of opening up shadow detail.

Result
The curve lightens the shadows, but holds the upper highlights.

Traditional curves

A more traditional approach is to go straight to the Curve window in the converter. In the latest ACR, four sliders below the curve target different tonal ranges, and here, the Darks slider has been used to raise the values of the second quarter of the range.

Vibrance

Vibrance is ACR's control for raising saturation without incurring clipping in any of the color channels.

Result

The version of the image completed using Adobe Camera Raw.

DxO

For comparison, the Raw conversion in DxO, making use of the before-and-after window. All of the same issues are addressed here as in Photoshop, but with different algorithms and in a different order. More than ACR, DxO is designed to be used in an automated way.

DOUBLE-PROCESSED RAW

A useful, if slightly time-consuming way of recovering the tonal range in a Raw image, is to process two versions — one for shadows, the other for highlights — and combine them.

In principle, the full range of a high-contrast image captured in a 12-bit or 14-bit Raw file can be compressed satisfactorily into an 8-bit viewable file using a Raw converter. The range of tools, including exposure, brightness, contrast, and curves adjustment, allow a great deal of control. However, most of these are global operators—tools that work on the entire range of tones and colors in the image—whereas many lowlight situations have, as we've seen, sharply divided areas of brightness. The problem is often that of maintaining local contrast while holding or reducing global contrast. Photoshop CS3's Recovery and Fill Light sliders do an excellent job of local control at different ends of the tonal scale, but in an image such as this, it may still be difficult to achieve a normal, natural-looking contrast in both the darker and lighter areas.

One way of overcoming this problem is to make two separate conversions of the Raw image and combine them later. In one version, ignore the shadow areas and concentrate on making the optimum adjustments for just the highlights and high middle tones (what Photoshop calls Highlights and Lights). In the second, do the reverse: concentrate only on the shadows and low middle tones (in Photoshop Shadows and Darks). This method borrows some of the techniques from multiple exposure blending—which normally requires a tripod (see pages 190-199)—but is well suited to single-shot handheld photography.

In normal Raw processing, and indeed in all normal Curves and Levels adjustments, the operations are biased towards the mid-tones. The most common of all adjustments to a histogram is a shift with its center in the middle. Points on the histogram or curve at a distance from the center are correspondingly weaker, with the shadows and highlights being affected least of all. Even if the center point of a shift is taken from lower or higher in the curve, the same principle applies. Global operations, which is what these are, affect the parts of the image that are usually the most important—the mid-tones—and have the advantage of being easy to understand and realistic in effect. However, if as in the image below, the important areas are in the shadows and/or highlights, it may be better to treat them separately.

Note that local operators such as Photoshop's Recovery and Fill Light adjustments are designed to tackle just this problem, and are very effective. They do, however, have one potential drawback, which is that because they work on local areas of pixels, they are not completely intuitive and can create unrealistic effects, particularly if aggressively used. The examples here show what can happen.

Best single Raw
The problem here is that there is interesting detail in the straw raincapes hanging close to the camera, yet even using Recovery and Fill in the raw converter fails to do justice to this while holding the bright reflections in the tin roof awning beyond.

Having made the two versions of the same image, the next step is to combine them. Here, contrary to what you might expect, there is a strong argument for doing this by hand with a large eraser brush, rather than procedurally. There are two reasons for this. First, the circumstances for choosing double-processed Raw are usually when you have spatially well-defined areas, which are therefore easier to choose with brushwork. Secondly, procedural blending methods do not discriminate between which areas of the image are adjusted.

Dual conversion
Instead, two Raw conversions are made, one concentrating only on the raincapes, the other only on the scene in the courtyard beyond.

Light

Layered and hand-erased
The darker version is pasted over the lighter, and partially erased with several strokes of a brush set to 40% opacity. This manual blending works because the area that needs treatment is well-defined and localized.

Dark

Final merged result
The result, equivalent (though by very different means) to traditional darkroom print-dodging.

DOUBLE-PROCESSED RAW

Highlight settings
You can save your highlight settings as a preset.

Raw default
This is the Auto result for the image, a reasonable compromise but with highlight clipping around the sun.

Raw adjusted
Even 100% Recovery of highlights does not fully restore the sun and its immediate surroundings. This treatment is rejected in favor of the Auto result.

Raw adjusted for highlights
The Raw file is processed a second time, concentrating on the highlights alone. The Exposure is reduced by 2.2 stops, Recovery increased by 100%, and a few other small adjustments made, including the Curve window. This second version is saved with a suffix "hi."

Basic and highlight
The two versions, with the detail around the sun compared. Note that good recovery of sun detail is achieved by simply lowering the exposure.

Curve adjustment

In an even more telling comparison, the darker version is lightened with a curve to the point where the roof in the detail is approximately the same value. The highlights remain much better.

Comp

The darker version is pasted over the normal, and blended in such a way as to favor its treatment of the sun, using Blending Options and the split highlight sliders.

HAND HELD HDRI

Under certain circumstances, this specialized technique for combining several different exposures in order to create one image that contains a wide range of brightness, can be used effectively without a tripod.

High Dynamic Range Imaging (HDRI) is the relatively new technique in which a series of different exposures, all of the same subject, are combined into a single, special file format that can encompass a much wider range of tones than a normal TIFF or JPEG. We deal with this more thoroughly in the next chapter, on pages 180-215, because it demands that all the image frames are in perfect register. This naturally makes it a technique for tripod shooting. However, recent improvements in automatic image alignment and is digital SLR camera design now make it feasible to attempt without a tripod.

For the full explanation of HDRI, see pages 194-195. In a way it is inconvenient to split up the subject between chapters, but unavoidable given that this is a hand held possibility, albeit specialized. For now, here is a brief summary of HDRI. Shooting a sequence of identically composed images that vary only in the shutter speed allows you to cover a potentially huge range of brightness. In this form it is, of course, useless, as it is spread across several images. However, there are now a number of special image file formats that can contain mathematically all the information in a single file. Known as 32-bit floating-point formats (see page 196 for a more detailed explanation), they can encode an almost infinite range of brightness, from deep shadow to details of light sources themselves. As ordinary camera sensors are incapable of capturing such a wide range in one go, the only practical possibility is to take a number of frames and then combine them into a single HDR file. This file must then be processed further in order to be able to produce a "normal" image file that can be viewed on a display monitor or in the form of a print, and this procedure, known as tonemapping, is discussed on page 200.

As each frame must be in perfect register for this to work, HDRI has been very much linked to tripod shooting. However, software that can generate HDR files from a sequence, including Photomatix Pro and Photoshop CS2 and CS3, now includes an automatic alignment feature, in which the images are analyzed for content and then shifted slightly in relation to each other as necessary. There are limits as to how well the auto-alignment can succeed, but there are no real difficulties with up to several pixels misalignment.

This brings us to the second part of the equation. One alternative to fixing the camera on a tripod in

SETTING UP AUTO BRACKETING

The bracketing sequence of 9 is set, with a maximum 1 fstop difference.

The mode chosen is Auto (A).

High-speed continuous is chosen for the shutter operation (Ch).

HAND HELD

order to shoot the sequence is to shoot very quickly, in a continuous burst. This minimizes the risk of moving the camera between frames. Some digital SLRs have an auto-bracketing function, and this can be turned into a useful way of shooting an HDR sequence. In the example here, the exposure bracketing is set up in advance on a Nikon D200. The highest step possible between frames is 1 f-stop, and the maximum number of frames is nine. While 2 f-stops is generally considered the most useful step between frames for generating an HDR file, 1 f-stop across 9 frames gives a total range of 8 f-stops, which is well adequate for most situations. Setting the camera to Continuous high speed mode allows a burst of 9 frames in as little as two seconds (this depends on the lighting conditions, as slower exposures add to the overall time). There should be little problem in holding the camera on the target for this short time, particularly if you are using a vibration-reduction lens. The main limit is the slower shutter speeds, with the risk of camera shake.

Hand held HDR
The sequence above begins with the best possible single frame, followed by the series of shots fed into the tonemapping tool. On the right is the aligned and mapped result.

PSEUDO-HDR

Some HDR software, notably Photomatix Pro and FDRTools, although not the current Photoshop, will import single Raw images for tonemapping. This is not, of course, true HDR, in that the range in a single Raw comes nowhere near the dynamic range that can be captured in a sequence of different exposures. Nevertheless, what makes this technique worth considering in lowlight photography is that the tonemapping procedures are sophisticated and powerful, and can often recover more from the shadows and highlights, as well as emphasizing local detail, than a normal Raw converter.

The powerful tonemapping algorithms in HDR software can be used on single Raw images to good effect; very useful with high-contrast images.

The example worked through here is processed in Photomatix Pro, which converts a Raw file into a pseudo-HDR file. In fact, the dynamic range of a Raw file depends only partly on the bit depth (typically 12-bits or 14-bits per channel). The file format at these bit depths is capable of storing a considerable dynamic range, but in practice this is much less, and is limited mainly by the sensor design, and specifically by the amount of noise present in the shadows. We'll see more of noise in the following pages, but the practical limit to the dynamic range of a single capture is the "noise floor," as it is called. This is easy to demonstrate if you open any image containing significant shadows in a Raw converter. As we saw on pages 120-123, modern Raw converters have ways of recovering information at both ends of the scale, but if you simply raise the exposure slider, at a particular level you will simply be revealing noise in the shadows, not real detail. This is the "noise floor" and sets the lower limit. The upper limit, naturally, is set by full exposure, which clips highlights to pure, featureless white.

As always, each image is different and specific, and has its own needs, and this is particularly so with lowlight shooting in which the shooting is usually pushing the limits. This photograph, shot at night on board a Thai fishing boat certainly presents a technical challenge. The only light for the captain at the wheel was a single bare lamp, but I liked the starkness of the lighting and the extreme play of light and shadow. Nevertheless, there was some doubt as to whether it would be possible to make a printable image.

JPEG Original
The accompanying JPEG shows the image as shot, not very promising. I always shoot Raw plus a basic JPEG, the latter for quick preview and mailing purposes.

STAGE 1: ADOBE CAMERA RAW

Highlight warning in Raw.

As a yardstick, the Raw file was first opened in Photoshop's Raw converter, and given as much recovery treatment as possible. This included 100% highlight Recovery, lowered Exposure, increased Fill Light, and increased Blacks. The result is still far from acceptable.

STAGE 2: PHOTOMATIX PRO

Your RAW file has been converted into a pseudo-HDR image.

Please note though that more than one exposure is needed to properly capture the dynamic range of most scenes. A good quality HDR image requires taking several exposures and combining them using "HDR->Generate."

The pseudo-HDR image is in 32 bits/channel mode. You can apply the Tone Mapping tool to it, but you can not combine it using the methods under the Combine menu.

OK

Note: You can disable the showing of this window in Preferences under the HDR tab.

Turning to a pseudo-HDR process, the Raw file is opened in Photomatix, which delivers this warning.

The large number of parameter sliders give many possibilities of tonemapping. This setting begins with the defaults, but then the Strength is increased.

Even with the many controls possible, no single tonemapping is ideal, and I decide to go one step further with this technique, and make more than one tonemapped version, with the intention of combining them later. In this second version, the S/H (shadow and highlight) controls are used strongly to recover and smooth.

STAGE 2: PHOTOMATIX PRO (CONTINUED)

Noise in the smooth shadow areas on the left of the image continues to be a problem, exaggerated by the very sliders that open up small-scale detail. For safety, I make a third version, this one aimed entirely at giving the least noise in these areas, ignoring the effect on the rest of the image. Highlights Smoothing and Shadows Clipping are turned off, and Shadows Smoothing increased to the maximum.

The three versions are combined in Photoshop, using layers, and hand-brushing with the Eraser. The main preferred version is on top, with the lighter open-shadow version underneath. The interior of the right window, and part of the center window behind the man's head are brushed through to reveal more detail. This done, these two layers are merged (Merge Visible), and the noisy areas in the shadows, particularly at left, are brushed away to reveal the less noisy version underneath. Finally, the layers are flattened.

STAGE 3: LIGHTZONE

The man's face appears too hot. The image is opened in LightZone to take advantage of its area selection method, drawing a bezier curve around the face while in White Balance.

The color temperature for this area is raised.

The result.

STAGE 4: NEAT IMAGE

Final work is on the noise, using Neat Image, a plug-in for Photoshop. Auto Profile is run.

After examining the noise at 100% magnification, and experimenting with different strengths, I decide that the tight noise structure is not particularly objectionable, and that the priority is sharp resolution on the face. Any excessive luminance noise reduction blurs this too much, so I settle for removing the chrominance noise.

The final result is a major improvement on any normal method of Raw processing.

TYPES OF NOISE

Noise is the digital equivalent of film grain, with fewer redeeming qualities, and is especially prominent in lowlight photography because of high sensitivity settings and slow shutter speeds.

Lowlight photography supplies the conditions for potentially noisy images. Indeed, there is no escape from the problem, because the two practical circumstances that create the most noise are high ISO settings and long exposures. Substituting hand held shooting for locked-down and vice versa simply exchanges different causes for the noise. And problem it certainly is because, while it invites comparison with film grain, it is aesthetically much less agreeable. The aesthetics of imagery are, of course, largely a matter of taste, but to date no photographer to my knowledge has chosen to use noise in a deliberate and positive way. With film, on the other hand, many photographers used the grain pattern from high-speed emulsions or enlargements of sections of film for texture and grittiness.

To understand why this is so, and also to help decide what actions to take in suppressing and removing noise, the purpose of these pages is to explain how noise originates and to examine its appearance in detail. Both film grain and noise are artifacts, but have different causes. The graininess of film is related to granularity, the random visible texture in a processed photograph that comes from the black silver grains from which the image is constructed (in black-and-white film). Fast films achieve their high sensitivity partly by increasing the size of the light-sensitive grains. The image in processed black-and-white film is in fact a mosaic of black silver grain clumps in a clear matrix, and so grain clumping is integral to the image. It is for this reason that film grain has usually been tolerated and even exploited for its graphic effect. One of the very few, or only, useful effects of noise is in suppressing discretization effects, such as banding. However, even this is better achieved for a more agreeable result by adding Gaussian noise, which has a clustered appearance.

With digital noise, the situation is different because in principle digital images are "clean." In practice, at low sensor sensitivity (ISO 100 to 200) and with plenty of light, the results are also clean. The appearance of noise in an image can be considered as a question of the efficiency of the sensor and the way the signal is processed. A close analogy is audible noise on a sound signal—crackling over a piece of music. Put another way, a digital photograph with less noise is more true to the original image projected by the lens, while a film photograph with less visible graininess simply has a tighter structure. The availability of numerous software filters to add the effect of film grain attests to its appeal, despite the dubious underlying logic.

There are several causes and therefore types of digital noise, but fundamentally it has to do with sampling errors. Photons of light are random, and the job of each photosite in a sensor is to convert them into electrons, which are then counted at the end of the exposure in the readout. Clearly, the more photons that fall across the sensor, the lower the sampling error will be. When it is darker, relatively few photons strike, so each has a greater effect on the photosite it affects. The upshot is that in shadow areas there is less chance that the photosites will make an accurate representation. This kind of noise, sometimes called "photon noise" may not be a problem if those deep shadow areas remain very dark, but opening them up in post-production will reveal them.

There are two ways of improving the photon count from dark areas. One is to increase the sensitivity of the sensor, the other to leave the sensor exposed to the light for longer so that more photons strike and a better average can be made. These two solutions, as you can see, are why the second half of this book is divided into two chapters: hand held for higher sensitivity and locked down for longer exposures. But each of these introduces another kind of noise.

Increasing the sensitivity of a sensor is done by increasing the gain of the readout amplifier. This is what happens when you dial up the ISO setting, and as in any electrical system, more amplifier gain means more noise, like static in a radio signal. Indeed, amplifier noise is the main culprit in the readout. This kind of noise is sometimes called "amp noise" or "readout noise" or "bias noise." Unlike photon noise, it is repeatable and predictable. As the only significant variable is the amplifier gain, this kind of noise can be treated by making a "noise profile" of a particular camera at a specific ISO setting, which we'll see in action on page 174.

A third kind of noise is known as "random noise," which in a sense is a catch-all term for the unpredictable and unrepeatable differences in the timing and behavior of different electronic components. It tends to increase with fast signal processing, and it is difficult to predict how much it contributes to the overall total. Advanced cameras usually take some internal steps toward suppressing it.

As mentioned above, increasing the exposure time is the other solution, but this brings into play another major contributor to noise, known as "dark noise." This is caused by imperfections in the sensor, and also by the addition of electrons to the photosite generated

Detail and noise
The blue box indicates an area of sharp focus and relative light where it is important to check for noise.

TYPES OF NOISE

by heat. In principle this can be reduced by cooling the sensor (as happens in astrophotography), but this is impractical in a normal camera. As a rough guide, a temperature increase of around 6-10°C doubles the amount of dark noise. Fortunately, this kind of noise is independent of the image, meaning that if you were to follow a long exposure with an identical second exposure with the lens cap on, you would have in the second frame an exact record of the same dark noise, which for this reason is also known as "fixed-pattern noise." This is the principle of "dark frame subtraction" which advanced cameras use (see pages 174). Dark noise also accumulates predictably over time, so that an exposure twice as long will have more or less twice the amount of noise. Practically, this is an issue for tripod photography rather than hand-held, but it seems more convenient to include it here in this general overview of noise.

In terms of appearance rather than cause, there are two main types of noise, luminance, and chrominance.

NOISE TYPES

Noise by cause	Noise by appearance
Photon noise	Random noise
Readout noise	Dark noise

Luminance noise appears as tonal fluctuations, and is usually the most prominent. In digital imaging, color actually contributes relatively little to the content, and you can check this for yourself by taking a noisy image in Photoshop and converting the Mode to Lab (*Image > Mode > Lab Color*). Lab color space uses a luminance channel and two color channels, a (red/ magenta to green) and b (blue to yellow). Zoom in to 100% on a noisy part of the image—in a relatively featureless area such as sky or flesh. Go to Channels

LUMINANCE NOISE

HAND HELD

Original

Luminance channel

144

and select each of the channels in turn. You will see that most of the noise—indeed, most of the subject detail also—is in the Luminance channel. Chrominance noise is less prominent, though where it does exist it is usually more disagreeable. It is related to the Color Filter Array over the sensor that interpolates the color information of the pixels; the "wrong" pixel information from noise tends towards one of the color channels.

In addition to all of this, noise goes beyond physics and into perception. This is extremely important when it comes to the reduction or removal of noise, and goes back to the definition of noise as an artifact. Even if noise exists in an image, we have to recognize it as such, and how does the eye and brain do that? Noise is random texture (spatial variations of tone and color), and at 100% magnification the only way to distinguish it from real subject detail is perceptually. This becomes hugely complex, as the brain must use familiarity, context, and expectations to decide. What this means

is that total noise removal from detailed areas of an image (where the level of detail is similar to that of the noise frequency) cannot be automated. In other words, all noise reduction needs your guidance as the user.

ARTIFACTS

Taken from its original meaning of a man-made object, an artifact in imaging is a visible data error introduced into the image by the process. It is thus separate in origin from the scene in front of the camera, and is a defect. Aesthetically there may be reasons for wanting to keep, alter, or enhance it, but from the point of view of the signal that generates the image it is an intruder. Both film grain and digital noise are artifacts. Analyzing the source of these artifacts for any particular image makes it possible to reduce their appearance without overly damaging the "true" image.

a channel

b channel

NOISE REDUCTION SOFTWARE

So far, I've concentrated on how noise occurs, what it looks like, and the problems of detecting it. With all types of noise reduction software, there are two principal steps. The first is detection, selecting those pixels considered to be rogue artifacts. The second, which we'll now look at, is the procedure for replacing them. At pixel level, noise is not simply removed,

A variety of algorithms exist for reducing noise, within image-editing programs, as plug-ins, and as dedicated standalone applications.

because that would leave a pattern of "holes," whatever their color. It has to be replaced with values that blend it into its surroundings. The simplest way is to use a blurring filter, which has the effect of smearing the pixel values over a chosen radius. A Gaussian Blur filter is the standard, default means of digital blurring, although for noise removal it is not necessarily the best choice. It works by averaging across the radius selected and, in the case of noise, pixels that are very different in tone from their surroundings may not smear them completely. A Median filter, however, works by selecting the most representative pixel in the group. So, for example, if in a selected area there are just black and white pixels, but slightly more of the black, a Gaussian filter will return a darker than average gray, while a Median filter will return black. The downside of a Median filter is that it can produce an artificial-looking "plastic" texture.

In either case, blurring by its nature destroys detail and reduces resolution, one of the essential problems of noise reduction. There are other methods. One is frequency analysis, using the Fourier transform, in which the image is converted into frequencies that are then searched for structures that do not conform to standard representations of edges and texture patterns. This method also has disadvantages, however, as frequency analysis sometimes incorrectly assumes patterns when none are present in reality, and so overcorrects by introducing strange textures. A more advanced form of frequency analysis uses wavelet transform, which enables the noise reduction to adapt to different noise conditions in different areas of an image.

As we saw on pages 10-15, noise is intimately related to demosaicing (the standard procedure that all Raw converters have to apply in order to reconstruct the colors from the Bayer filter over the camera's sensor). So, better ways of demosaicing, meaning more sophisticated algorithms, can significantly reduce noise by doing a better job of identifying it. A good example of this is the latest version of DxO Optics Pro (version 5), in which the demosaicing algorithm searches up to several tens of pixels around each one in order to find patterns and consistencies. In this way it more easily finds the inconsistencies that represent noise, and suppresses them rather than enhances (which is what primitive Raw converters do).

The blurring problem is one aspect of a more fundamental issue that I already touched on—how to distinguish and remove noise only from the areas where it is objectionable. Ultimately this is a personal, subjective assessment. One researcher's comment was "one person's noise is another person's signal." And, as Jim Christian, Noise Ninja's developer, explains, noise reduction is essentially heuristic, meaning the methods work largely by trial and error. In the end, whatever noise reduction method you use, you should be able to choose where on the image it is applied. Fortunately, one common principle applies to most viewers and most images, and this is that noise is most apparent in areas of an image that are otherwise smooth and lacking in detail. This becomes obvious when you examine an image such as this, which contains the four-way contrast of in-focus detail, out-of-focus detail, in-focus featureless subject, and out-of-focus featureless subject. Well-designed software can locate otherwise detail-free areas and apply more aggressive noise reduction to these, while protecting areas of fine detail. There are limits to how efficiently this can be done, so that it is important to add your own, user decisions to the process. Some noise reduction software allows this, but even if not, you can

NOISE NINJA

Original image

The default settings. As the lower window shows, the camera and ISO setting has been recognized, and the pre-loaded profile applied.

The default settings can now be checked and tweaked according to taste and the image, using the Noise Ninja recommended procedure, as follows. Step one is to raise Strength to maximum.

Smoothness is then set to zero.

Smoothness is raised until just below the point where speckling becomes noticeable.

Finally, Strength is lowered until the balance between detail and smoothness is to your taste.

Sharpening, always intimately connected to noise, is then adjusted to taste.

Corrected image

NOISE REDUCTION SOFTWARE

at least use Layers or some other non-destructive method to fade or restore the filter's effects selectively. Selective sharpening in one form or another is essential.

While the better programs apply noise reduction selectively, the way in which they do it is not always transparent, meaning that you are largely taking the developer's word for it that this is being handled efficiently. Until you have settled on one program and use this regularly, it remains important to check the results of the filter, as always at 100%. Again, some programs facilitate this (Noise Ninja, for example has a single button that toggles backward and forward between the uncorrected and corrected states), but if not, it may be worth running the noise reduction on a duplicate layer if the filter is available as a Photoshop plug-in, or copying the corrected image onto the uncorrected original in Photoshop. Toggling the upper layer off and on is effective at showing the results, detail by detail. Areas that you feel have been treated too aggressively can then be easily retouched by partial erasing.

As a result of the many variables in the creation of noise, the different ways of reducing it, and its perceptual nature, it is hardly surprising that there are many software applications for dealing with it, each with its own characteristics. Currently there are more than twenty consumer applications, although only a few cross-platform. As each requires user input, making comparisons is unreliable, not to mention time-consuming. Here we show a few cross-platform programs, one of which is inevitably a filter in Photoshop. Do not take the comparisons shown here as absolute references — the differences have as much to do with the particular images and my own choices in applying the effects as the design of the software.

CASE STUDY: ISO 1000 NOISE REDUCTION

This shot, of a small squid fishing boat on a sandbank in Thailand, is very much on the edge of technical acceptability. Taken hand-held from a moving boat well after dusk, it was one of the very few of a set of 16 frames in which the main subject was sharp. The shutter speed was 1/8 sec, which was highly optimistic shooting at 93 mm efl (even though this was a Nikon Vibration Reduction lens). The sensitivity was set to ISO 1000, which always delivers pronounced noise. To hold the color of the green fluorescent striplight (used for attracting the squid), I took the precaution of underexposing the rest of the image, which prevented clipped highlights but laid up trouble later for noise. The Raw converter would certainly be able to pull up the shadows, but at the cost of a very noisy image, as the noise is more pronounced in the dark shadows.

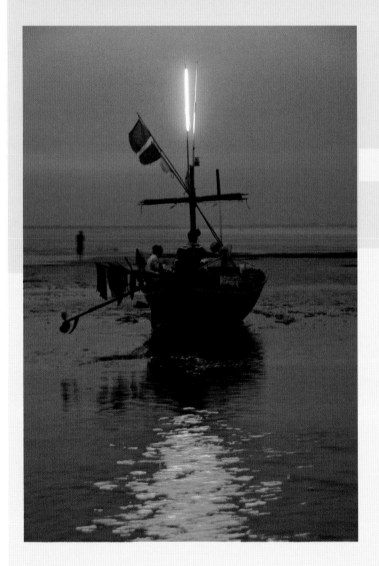

STAGE 1: ADOBE CAMERA RAW

Noise reduction in Photoshop's Raw converter, adjusted by eye for the optimal result.

STAGE 2: NEAT IMAGE

The noise reduction procedure in Neat Image begins with Auto Profiling. The program automatically seeks a smooth area, in this case the sky.

The automated default settings previewed on a key area of detail.

Luminance (Y) raised 15% to 75%

Luminance (Y) lowered 15% to 45%

The luminance noise default reduction of 60% shown for comparison lowered and raised by 15%.

NOISE REDUCTION SOFTWARE

Noise reduction introduces a workflow issue, because of the different approaches taken by different software, and this is particularly crucial if you are shooting Raw. If you are satisfied with the noise reduction performance built in to your primary Raw converter or image editing program, then the decision is straightforward—simply apply it during the Raw conversion or, if the image is a TIFF or JPEG, as soon as you open it. Whatever means are used by the software to judge and the reduce noise, it works more reliably when the image has been least altered.

However, the several independent noise-reduction programs, as we've just seen, lay claim to doing the job better. Before anything else, then, it is important to try out the various choices and decide for yourself which you prefer. There is a strong element of personal preference in this, as noise reduction is not a "clean" procedure. It always carries some side effects, and there are trade-offs between efficiency and final appearance, on which only you can decide. Then again, speed of processing in batches may be more important to you than spending more time on individual images. And, even taking both these factors into account, you are likely to find that some images respond better to one noise-reduction software than others.

As with blur repair, there are two stages followed by noise reduction filters. First, the noise has to be analyzed. Then a particular algorithm has to be applied that reduces the variation in tone and color between the noisy pixels and their neighbors. Different noise reduction software has different algorithms, and this more than anything accounts for differences in the final image appearance. There is an element of taste and judgement here, both on the part of the software developer and the user. Complete noise removal from a zone of the image may also give it a plastic-like, artificial texture—or rather, an absence of texture.

STAGE 3: NOISE NINJA

1. *The image as opened in Noise Ninja. At this stage, the profile is either loaded (as here, from the library), or created from analyzing the image.*

4. *Smoothness is then raised until just below the point where speckling becomes obvious.*

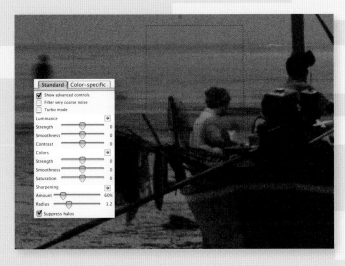

2. The Noise Ninja default settings.

3. Basic Strength/Smoothness adjustment begins with raising Strength to maximum.

5. Then Strength is reduced to taste.

The results, compared side by side, with, from left to right, the Raw default without noise correction in Photoshop ACR, with noise correction in Photoshop ACR, Neat Image, and Noise Ninja. This shows that it is less a matter of better of worse, more a trade-off between less noise and maintaining realistic detail.

NOISE REDUCTION SOFTWARE

There are side effects, of which this "plastic" appearance is one. Another is softness, because reducing sharpness is inevitably part of noise reduction. Distinguishing between featureless, smooth areas and those containing detail is difficult to automate. As we already saw, in some areas of some images, noise is indistinguishable from detail.

Noise reduction software that depends on camera-sensitivity modules prepared by the software manufacturer and loaded up in advance absolutely needs the purest image data to work on. There may well be a dilemma here, in that the noise-reduction software (Noise Ninja is one example of this kind) will work better if you do little to the image during the preceding Raw conversion, whereas Raw conversion now offers more and more attractive procedures for optimizing the image in other ways, such as lightening shadows and recovering highlights. My best advice is to run a few tests, contrasting minimum-alteration Raw processing against full alteration, both followed by noise reduction. Judge the results at high magnification, at least 100 percent. Note that "dark frame subtraction" procedures, being repeatable, are usually best performed either in-camera or with the Raw converter, and specific noise-reduction programs such as Noise Ninja or Neat Image work very well afterwards to take care of the other kinds of noise.

Detail of the image, processed as a TIFF from Raw without any noise reduction.

Luminance channel

a channel

b channel

Noise reduction in Photoshop ACR, maximum for both Luminance and Color, with a small amount of sharpening.

Converting the TIFF RGB to Lab mode, then viewing the channels separately, shows that, as usual, most of the noise is concentrated in the luminance channel.

NOISE REDUCTION SOFTWARE

NEAT IMAGE

Default analysis (Auto Profile)

NOISE NINJA

In Noise Ninja, the library profile for this ISO setting and camera is loaded.

The square preview area is chosen by clicking on the image, here chosen to show its effect on the face. These are the default settings.

RESULTS

Neat Image

Noise Ninja

Filtering (60% luminance)

The profiling re-directed to the face, which is the more important area, and the filtering adjusted to taste (50% luminance).

Strength is increased, with a slight decrease in Smoothness.

In Noise Ninja, the library profile for this ISO setting and camera is loaded.

PSR removed

with Noise

ADDING FLASH

While full flash effectively replaces lowlight photography, judiciously adding a small amount to the normal exposure is a valuable technique.

Strictly speaking, lowlight photography is about shooting without the aid of photographic lights, of which even a built-in camera flash is one. Nevertheless, it really depends to what extent you use it to shape the final image, and among the most common techniques is to add a relatively small amount of flash to the end of an exposure otherwise metered for the ambient conditions. This rear-curtain flash technique is well-established, and most digital SLRs have a setting that allows it. Briefly, the flash is computed to fire at the end of the exposure, as the final curtain of the focal plane shutter is closing, rather than at the beginning or during. This is an important distinction for any shot that is at a relatively slow shutter speed (say, slower than 1/30 sec), because motion blur, either from the camera or the subject or both, will create streaking, while the flash freezes everything sharply. Clearly, if the flash is at the start, the streaking will continue on from this, and if it is somewhere in the middle of the exposure the image will be even more confusing, with streak tracks on either side of the sharp details. The strongest case is for the flash terminating the entire exposure; most images are more legible this way.

The principle of combining lowlight streaking with a flash-frozen punctuation is that the two quite different visual effects complement each other. Arguably the most effective balance is when the main component is the lowlight streaking, with the flash providing just enough exposure to "close" the image and make sense of what might otherwise be moving details that are hard to understand. Personal preference, of course, is a major factor, and the only way to decide on your ideal combination is to try out several for yourself. There are clearly many permutations of shutter speed and flash strength, and these are affected also by the situation and content. To list just a few, there is the amount of subject movement, the basic readability of the subject (some things just don't make sense unless they are sharp and clear), whether the subject is light in tone against a dark background or the opposite, and the color balance of the ambient lighting (orange tungsten makes a strong contrast with white flash). If there is time to prepare, run a few different combinations of shutter speed and flash amount to see which appears to work best. There are usually several choices of camera setting to balance and combine these two; there's no reason to list these here as they vary by make and model and are fully detailed in the camera's instruction manual.

Rear-curtain flash

A sugar-cane cutter finishing his shift before dawn in Sudan. The ideal balance sought, and achieved here after experimenting with different flash/exposure combinations, was dark enough to convey the atmosphere of pre-dawn, a hint of tone in the sky, and some effect from the man's head-lamp. In addition, good depth of field for this close, 33mm efl wide-angle shot (the camera was held out to the ground) demanded a small aperture (f 16) and therefore a high ISO setting. The flash exposure bias was -0.7 and shutter speed 1/10 sec.

FLASH ANGLE

Depending on positioning, flash units can make dramatically different looking images. Here are some alternate results from the same shot, and plan views of the setup required.

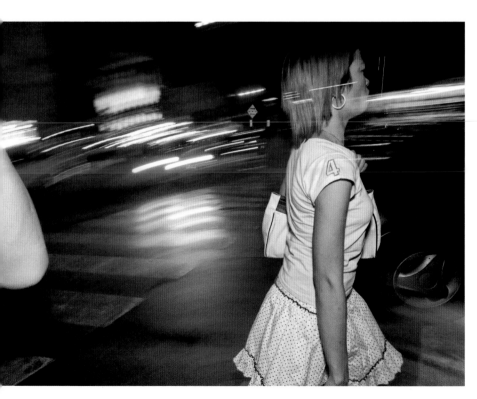

LEFT **Rear curtain flash**
Here, the on-camera flash is used at full strength (exposure bias 0.0) and slow speed (1/13 sec), so that the figure is well-exposed, while car headlights behind are bright enough to create streaking patterns from the pan. ISO 1600, f6.3, and a wide-angle 18mm efl.

BELOW
Remote flash for effect
Off-camera and triggered remotely (or as in this case held by a companion out of sight), flash can also be used as a practical light, simply for effect. Here, a single flash is used to add a little atmosphere to a moonlit shot of pyramids. Exposure time 30 sec at f2.8 and ISO 400.

ADDING FLASH

SECTION 3
LOCKED DOWN

Lowlight photography embraces many subjects and situations, from highly-charged down-town city streets at night to silent evening landscapes. In the last chapter we looked at what is for the most part a reportage approach to photography, suited to subjects that move, unpredictable moments that need quick reaction, and a way of working that is light on equipment and carries a percentage of failed shots.

But when the main subject remains still, or reasonably so, and you have more than a few seconds to get ready for a shot, the more reliable technique is to use a tripod, or some equivalent means of locking down the camera. This simple act opens the way for long exposures that can handle almost any light level, and some guarantee that the shot will be technically fine, meaning sharp, accurately exposed, and with noise kept under control. Some of the newest technical developments, especially in the processing stage with techniques like HDRI (High Dynamic Range Imaging) can make a quite remarkable difference, enabling results that would have been inconceivable without digital technology.

There is, as we'll see, rather more technology involved (or at least available to us) in locked-down photography than in hand-held, and more of it concentrated in post-production. Nevertheless, while the process of shooting is certainly more reliable than hand-held, it demands its own particular technical proficiency. There is more equipment to carry in the form of the tripod, and that alone establishes a different approach. In place of the physical attention that hand-held photography demands, there is care in tripod management and protection from vibration—demands that have not, of course, changed throughout the history of photography. What is new is the need to plan ahead at the time of shooting, making exposures that will in many cases undergo considerable post-production.

TRIPODS

TRIPODS

However proficient you become at hand-held shooting, a solid, locked camera support is still the most secure technique for shooting. It is essential for any lighting condition that puts the fastest shutter speed below the safe limit for the combination of lens focal length and hand steadiness. Tripods, in various forms and designs, are the basic mechanical support. Rigidity is paramount, though for ease of carrying around this often has to be compromised to some extent by the tripod's portability. Increasingly, new materials, such as

The huge range of tripods available reflects the different priorities of stability, weight, bulk, and cost, and also varied usage according to the situation and subject.

carbon fiber and basalt fiber are being used, which have a higher strength-to-weight ratio than traditional metal alloys, so are light, while remaining rigid, but are considerably more expensive.

The standard portable design has telescopic legs, usually in three sections, a rising center column for fine adjustments, and a fixed angle of spread. There are many variations as manufacturers compete for attention. A variable angle of spread has advantages in that you can accommodate different surfaces, but this usually involves an extra set of bars with sliding collars (these are standard for professional filming and video, where weight is not such an issue as in still photography). An alternative is a second fixed position (Gitzo use this extensively). A wide spread can also be useful for a lower camera position, and better stability in windy conditions.

Quick setup tripod
The Manfrotto 458B Neotec tripod is fast and easy to use, with an innovative Neotec rapid opening and closing mechanism—just pull each leg downwards to open and automatically lock it in any position, with no screws, knobs, or levers to tighten or loosen. To fold it back up again, press the release button and push the leg closed.

Flat tripod
The Cullman Universal Magic tripod has the ability to fold each leg flat for portability.

Multipod
The Cullmann 3080 Multipod can be braced both against the ground and walls other available upright at the same time.

Gitzo
The G1158T Tripod is a simple and classic design from manufacturer Gitzo.

Foot or Spike
Tripod with changeable foot or spike.

Aluminum tripod
Sturdy aluminium legs make this tripod firm but heavier than some other models.

TRIPODS

Piccolo
Cullman's ultra-portable tripod, which folds up smaller than a packet of cigarettes.

Cullman Moskito
A portable mini-tripod which features a two way pan head.

Novoflex
This mini tripod design has legs which can be moved to different holes in the head for convenience.

Table top tripod
A small table top tripod combines portability with rigidity, when you don't need an eye-level viewpoint.

Gitzo GT2530
The ideal support for fluid heads. It introduces a new degree of integration between head and tripod: the leveling tripod sets the camera perfectly horizontal while the fluid head allows pan and tilt movements.

Carbon fiber tripod
The lightest tripods are build with carbon fiber, like this Manfrotto 055MF3, which is designed to take the strain of outdoor use while being as light to carry as possible.

MARKET INNOVATION

As the behavior and tolerances of synthetic materials are better understood, more and more versatile products are emerging, like the Gorillapod, which has flexible legs that can be bent around any convenient support, or used in traditional mini-tripod form.

Quick setup tripod

The Manfrotto Triaut tripod features patented simultaneous release of all three legs or any individual leg. This permits the legs to be extended, the tripod levelled (spirit level provided), and locked in seconds without "fiddling" with individual leg adjustments. The arms attaching the base of the central support to the legs make this tripod especially sturdy.

TRIPOD MANAGEMENT AND TECHNIQUES

There is a surprisingly big difference in stability between a tripod used well and one set up inefficiently. Tripods obey the laws of mechanics, and the aim in setting up is for maximum stability. This is largely a quest for rigidity, and there are a number of ways you can help. A tripod's telescopic legs are more stable when compact than when extended, which means that a tripod at its most compact on a solid raised ledge (or other surface) will be steadier than the same tripod extended from the ground. Equally, when you extend a telescopic leg, extend the thicker sections before the thinner ones.

The effectiveness of a tripod at stabilizing a camera depends as much on how you use it as on the tripod design and construction.

The surface on which the tripod is erected also matters. Outdoors, beware of sand and any loose conglomerate like pebbles. If in doubt, twist and press the feet down to make sure they are on as stable a surface as possible. Grass and earth, even though soft, can be good, provided that the feet can be pressed in—a spiked foot is an advantage. Remember that outdoors the tripod must also battle the wind, which is especially troublesome if it is gusty. Indoors, carpets are notoriously spongy and uncertain, and bare wooden floorboards can shift if trodden on, even some distance from the tripod.

The tripod is at its most stable when the head is exactly centered between the three feet which it sites above, and when the platform, immediately below the head, is level. Some models have a spirit level built into the platform. Try and level this rather than levelling only by means of the head. For the same reasons, try and ensure that the combination of camera and lens has its center of gravity over the center of the tripod. That's why long lenses have threaded mounts.

You can test the stability by gently tapping the end of the lens. Look for any visible movement of the equipment, then repeat this tapping while looking through the viewfinder. As mentioned, you can improve the stability of the set-up by lowering the center of gravity of the tripod plus camera. One additional way of doing this is to add a weight to the center; a few tripods have a hook at the base of the center column for this purpose. Hang anything you have handy, even your camera bag.

Tripod maintenance involves keeping the collars and other parts of the telescopic leg system clean, dry, free of abrading particles, and lubricated appropriately. Molybdenum disulfide and graphite are high-quality lubricants often used by manufacturers, but it also pays to find out exactly what the tripod manufacturer recommends. Also keep the joints at optimum tightness—not so tight that they are difficult to move, but without any play or sideways movement.

TRIPOD SET-UP CHECKLIST

- The shorter the legs, the more stable
- Extend thicker leg sections first
- Choose a solid surface
- Level the tripod platform
- Aim for the center of gravity of camera and lens over the center of the tripod
- Shelter from wind
- Add weight for stability

TRIPOD EQUIPMENT

Tripod central hook
Used to hang bags, as shown, from the central column.

Super telephoto
This Nikon lens has a center of gravity much nearer the front, hence the support, which should be mounted onto a tripod rather than using the camera's own mount.

Tripod bag
Use a camera bag to add weight and stability to a tripod setup.

Roller bag
This LowePro rolling camera bag includes a convenient set of straps to keep a tripod save.

Tripod bag
This LowePro camera bag includes a tripod holder making carrying of a full sized tripod far easier.

MONOPODS

More Stable

Less stable

HEADS: RANGE OF MODELS

There are two basic designs of tripod head, but many individual designs, and some crossovers. The most traditional is a pan and tilt head, with each axis of movement kept mechanically separate (roll, pitch, and yaw, if you like). The entire assembly rotates at the base, and this can be locked, usually with a screw knob. Two locking arms each control one of the other movements. Rotation, of course, is 360°, and the advantage of this tried and tested design is that small adjustments can be made in a single direction without upsetting the others. This is important if you need to level the camera precisely.

The choice of tripod head is every bit as crucial as the tripod itself; this is the all-important interface between the camera and support.

Ball-and-socket heads, normally referred to as ball heads, have become increasingly popular, partly because they can be switched between locked and completely free very quickly, and partly because they are very compact, adding very little size to the folded profile of the tripod. For situations that call for solid support at some times, but free movement at others, ball heads have a clear advantage. When slightly loosened, they are ideal for following subject movement, though heads designed for videographers have some advantages in this area.

TRIPOD HEADS

Off-center ball
An off-center ball head allows a different range of movements from the conventional center-ball design. Here it is combined with a separate pan control.

Three-way head
*Made of light magnesium
alloy, this typical three-way
head offers three independent
axes of motion, each with a
locking handle/lever. The best
brands use fluid cartridges
for accurate movement
with minimal effort.*

Attachment
*A tripod with a
three-way head
fitted to it.*

Ball heads
*Increasingly popular for being compact and
very quick to use, feature a single locking
mechanism. The single disadvantage, which
may not be important, is that releasing the
lock means re-setting the camera completely,
rather than being able to keep one or two
axes aligned, as with a 3-way head.*

Quick Release
*Quick-release systems, this one from
Manfotto, are an essential part of any
quick-response tripod shooting. The
base attaches to the tripod head, and
individual plates to the camera(s).*

HEADS: RANGE OF MODELS

Video head
Video heads like this pan and tilt often have a dampened, fluid-filled head to allow for smooth movement. The mount is the same as for a stills camera, however, so they can be used in a locked position if that is all there is to hand.

Panorama head
Marked for accurate positioning, a panoramic head is specifically designed for shooting images to be stitched into panoramas.

Cut away
The inner workings of a ball head and rack.

Geared head
Designed for accurate camera movement.

Gimbal head
This Wimberley gimbal head is designed for long lens attachments like that shown on page 167.

Adjustable plate
Fine measurements can be used in macro photography.

CLAMPS AND ALTERNATIVES

PORTABLE EQUIPMENT

There are many alternative solutions to tripods for securing a
camera, adapted to different shooting situations and viewpoints.

Cullmann touring aet
*Features in a single box a mini-tripod,
suction pad, ground spike, universal
clamp and woodscrew. All of these
items can be extended using the center
column and ball-and-socket head of
the mini-tripod.*

Woodscrew
*A woodscrew with ¼-inch
thread connection. Can be
screwed into beams, fence
posts, and tree stumps.*

Universal clamp
*For secure mounting to round,
square or irregularly shaped
objects. Can also be fitted to
some tripod heads and columns.
With a ¼-inch thread connection.*

Suction pad
*Activated by a U-shaped lever,
grips on any smooth surface
such as glass, marble, metal,
or plastic, and takes a load
up of up to 6 lbs (3 kg).*

Ground spike
*For pushing into any ground
like sand, earth, pebbles,
snow etc. It combines with
a ball-and-socket head.*

Cullmann Clamp Magic
*Especially design to be
attached to round or
irregularly shaped objects.*

Suction clamp
*A suction pad with a clamp
for holding reflectors and
other loads.*

Novofex car window accessory set
*Featuring an accessory plate with a
screw thread for connection of a ball
and socket head or other accessories.
Rigidity is achieved by the additional
support obtained from a monopod or
the Novoflex Chestpod.*

LOCKED DOWN

SLR supported
Clamping to toughened glass can be surprisingly effective, even with quite heavy cameras.

Carry case
The car accessory set can be kept neatly in this case.

Camera in place
The ball head allows camera movement when attached to a clamp, ideal for angled windows like those on most cars.

Clamp and rod set
This versatile set handles all of the situations shown on this page, and more.

Clamp and head
A clamp attached to a piece of glass, with ball head mounted to it.

Clamp
A simple clamp, as used above.

Clamp and rod
Additional height can be achieved when a clamp is used in conjunction with a rod.

Bar mount
The indent in the clamp means it can also be attached to a circular rod, like a handlebar.

MOTION BLUR WITH TRIPODS

Motion blur with the camera mounted on a tripod allows much greater control than when hand-held, and gives two distinct possibilities. One is subject motion blur with the camera motionless, so that the setting remains sharp. The other is smooth panning, and if you have time to set up a tripod, this assumes some kind of predictable, or at least anticipated, subject. We looked at panning and tracking on pages 124-125, and while either works well enough hand-held, using a tripod offers two advantages. One is that it frees at least one hand to operate camera controls, the other is that it allows a steadier flow of movement. In either case, subjects that have distinct blocks of tone or color, and an outline that is easy to recognize, tend to convert well into a motion-blurred image. Using a tripod makes it possible to work with quite long exposures, such as one second or more, although the mirror-up position makes following a subject at these speeds a little unpredictable.

A word about the tripod head. Ideally, there should be enough friction to support the camera and lens without putting strain on your hands, and with enough free play in the direction of the pan to follow the target without drag effects. As most panning sequences involve horizontal movement, it usually helps to loosen the rotating axis fully, keeping the friction quite firm on the other movements. This depends on the kind of

> **Expect different characteristics of image smearing and streaking when the camera is locked down from when you hold it freely by hand.**

READABILITY

This sequence of images, with a figure clad in black walking repeatedly in front of an art installation, was shot at 1/3 sec. The shutter speed was determined in advance by experiment — sufficient to show that it is a walking figure, but as motion-blurred as possible to emphasise the ambiguity of the scene. The basic problem is that the movement of the legs in certain positions (most positions, in fact) makes the figure look one-legged. In cases such as these, it is important to shoot sufficient frames for a good choice. Here, the third frame of the four "reads" best.

LOCKED DOWN

head. For instance, some ball-and-socket heads have an additional rotational movement; a good panning set-up with this type is medium friction on the ball and loose on the rotation. If there is no additional rotational movement available then you will need the ball to be set looser.

One danger in tripod panning is that if the tripod itself is not level, the vertical and horizontal smear lines in the image from motion blur will become increasingly askew as the camera is rotated. If you have time to prepare the setup and know in advance the route that the moving subject will follow, check the moving view through the viewfinder with a quick practice run first. Another reason for checking out the path of the pan is that it may involve changes in focus and exposure. Most lenses are now autofocus, but for ones that are not, you will need to continually check and adjust the focus during the pan. Almost all modern SLRs have focusing features for just such situations as these, and can make some prediction of distance as the camera follows the subject. This is known as AI Servo on Canon cameras, for example, and can be quickly set via the camera buttons.

Enlivening without detracting

One practical use of motion blur with the tripod locked down is when the subject is inherently not particularly interesting. In this case, a photograph was needed of the entrance to this office, but to give it some extra interest, the shot was timed for the moment when a visitor was leaving. Setting a shutter speed of 1/4 sec made the person less recognizable, and blurred the figure to make it less prominent.

LONG-EXPOSURE NOISE

A specific kind of noise occurs at long exposures, particularly in the region of several seconds and more, related to the characteristics and defects of each individual sensor.

As touched on earlier, "dark" or "fixed-pattern" noise is caused by imperfections and irregularities in the sensor, including, for example, uneven boosting between the individual readout amplifiers accompanying each photosite on a CMOS sensor. It increases approximately in proportion to the exposure time, and at one or several minutes can be very noticeable. It is also enhanced by heat-generated electrons adding to the photosites, so you can expect more noise in warm weather than in cold. Because this kind of noise is related to the sensor and its circuitry and not to the image, it lends itself to fairly efficient correction. The key, however, is to record the exact pattern of the noise at the time of shooting. Some cameras, generally the more advanced DSLRs, have a menu option to do this automatically and make an immediate reduction of the noise, and the results are usually impressive. The main drawback is that it adds the same amount of time again as the original exposure, and if you allowing a few minutes for an exposure, this may not be acceptable.

The procedure is known as "dark frame subtraction," and even with simpler cameras you can take this essential step for later noise reduction. You shoot a "dark frame" immediately after the shot, without changing any settings at all, and the simple way is to use a lens cap, also covering or locking up the viewfinder if there is any light falling on the camera

NOISE INCREASES WITH RAW ADJUSTMENTS

As Exposed
Noise is well suppressed with the Raw image converted to TIFF at standard settings, without any adjustment to either the exposure or the brightness.

Corrected
This area of the image, with an area of moonlit sand visible, shows what happens when the Exposure slider in Photoshop ACR is raised by 2 stops. The result is serious noise, which would need to be addressed in post-production.

Original
This night shot, with a full moon rising behind pyramids in the Nubian desert, was was exposed at 15 sec at an aperture of f3.5 and a low ISO of 200. The clarity of the atmosphere accounts for the high level of brightness and thus relatively short exposure (see pages 38-47). Long-exposure in-camera noise reduction was on. Nevertheless, while this combination of settings works well for an image as exposed, noise problems still appear when attempts are made to open detail from the shadow areas.

THE EFFECTS OF IN-CAMERA REDUCTION

A sequence of 5 exposures shot under failing daylight at the end of the day, at auto exposure and the same low sensitivity of ISO100, in order. In-camera long-exposure noise reduction kicks in at shutter speeds of one second and slower, and for these longer exposures the shot was taken with and without this in-camera reduction, to make a comparison.

1/8 sec

1/4 sec

1 sec

4 sec

15 sec

NOISE COMPARISON

noise reduction on   noise reduction off

2 *f*-stops underexposed, corrected in Raw

noise reduction on   noise reduction off

Correct aperture setting

Noise Comparison

Perhaps surprisingly, the difference between noise-reduction on and off is quite subtle, even at the long exposure of one minute shown here in this side-by-side comparison. The top pair is a comparison between on (left) and off (right). To highlight the effect, a deliberate underexposure of two stops on the aperture was corrected in Raw conversion. The lower pair is the same, save that the exposure is correct. The difference between on and off is slightly more obvious on the upper pair. More importantly, adjustments in the Raw conversion (or with a TIFF by raising the gamma in Levels or Curves) has a more damaging effect than not choosing in-camera reduction.

LONG-EXPOSURE NOISE

from behind. So, for example, if the original exposure is 1 minute at f11 and ISO 200, use exactly these settings a second time with the lens tightly covered. As shown here, this "dark frame" can then be combined with the normal frame in Photoshop to reduce the pixel pattern that they have in common. Note that this will not work with a JPEG because of the large amount of in-camera processing that happens immediately after readout to compress the image, as this alters the data drastically.

DIY DARK FRAME CAPTURE

The first step of this procedure is to shoot the dark frame; follow this in post-production with the subtraction.

1. Set the camera to Raw format.

2. Turn in-camera noise reduction and sharpening off. Sharpening in some cameras does indeed affect the Raw file, contrary to general expectations.

3. Set the ISO, shutter speed and aperture and, if the camera is set to Auto, remember them.

4. Shoot.

5. Place the lens cap over the lens, and unless you are in extreme darkness, shield the camera from light (such as in the shoulder bag or covered with a jacket).

6. If the camera was set to Manual, simply take a second identical exposure. If the camera was on Auto, turn it to Manual, and set the shutter speed and aperture to those just used and shoot.

DARK FRAME SUBTRACTION

As all good cameras now use dark frame subtraction as the basis of in-camera long-exposure noise reduction, it is not necessary to do this manually. Nevertheless, for interest, a dark frame is shown here, shot at 60 sec at the same time as the sequence of masks on a wall shown on the previous page. The noise is usually invisible, without exaggeration on the dark frame, but by dragging the white point slider in Levels to just above the minimum (level 2), and magnifying at 100%, the fixed pattern noise can be seen.

Levels adjusted to just above minimum.

DIY DARK FRAME SUBTRACTION

Once the dark frame is captured (left) there are many ways of performing the subtraction. The following is one method in Photoshop. Please bear in mind that there are many potential problems.

1. Open both images (original image and dark frame) in Raw converter software.

2. Set identical white balance for each.

3. Make no other changes, in particular no clipping and no sharpening.

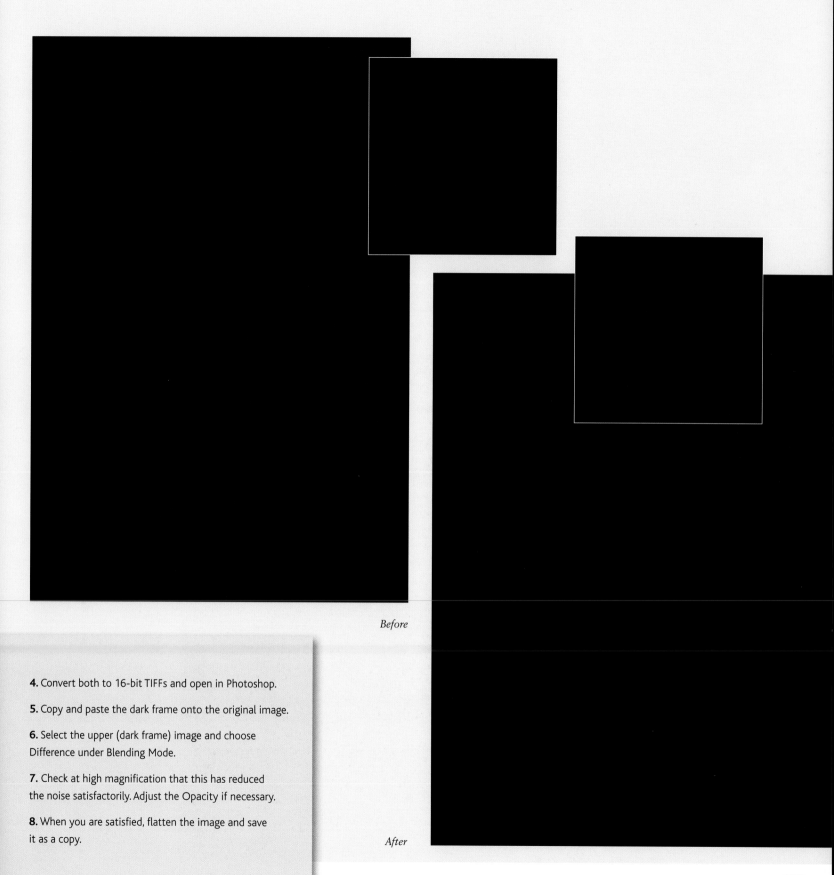

Before

4. Convert both to 16-bit TIFFs and open in Photoshop.

5. Copy and paste the dark frame onto the original image.

6. Select the upper (dark frame) image and choose Difference under Blending Mode.

7. Check at high magnification that this has reduced the noise satisfactorily. Adjust the Opacity if necessary.

8. When you are satisfied, flatten the image and save it as a copy.

After

IMAGE AVERAGING FOR NOISE

While fixed pattern noise and, to an extent, readout noise are amenable to in-camera treatment, "random noise" is intractable. By its nature it is completely unpredictable, and it is also difficult to gauge how much it contributes to the overall noise in any given situation. In the final image, the different sources of noise are overlaid on each other. However, there exists an effective, though time-consuming method of isolating and reducing "random noise" on a picture by picture basis.

Making a series of exposures consecutively and with identical settings creates a set of frames in which the only difference is random noise, which can then be reduced or removed

This is the image averaging technique, and calls for a few or several identically framed shots taken consecutively. Because it needs to be planned for, and drastically slows down shooting, it is not likely to become a standard technique. It can be performed only with the camera locked on a tripod, because the frames must be in pixel-perfect register.

The principle is that if the scene is completely still, without any subject movement, the only variable between identically exposed frames will be the random noise. Averaging the images removes this noise. In astrophotography this is a well-known technique, and it applies equally to regular lowlight photography. In practice, it means repeating the shot without any movements to the camera, taking special care with the tripod and shutter release. No special software is needed other than Photoshop, because the averaging is done with layers. Photoshop CS3 has a feature called image stacks which makes the procedure very much easier. Like Dark Frame Subtraction to reduce dark or fixed-pattern noise, it increases the signal-to-noise ratio of the image and so is non-destructive, unlike most software methods which blend noisy pixels into their local neighborhood. The noise between two frames is averaged, in effect reducing it by half in the combined image. This is more or less the equivalent of noise from half the ISO setting.

In Photoshop CS2 or earlier, copy and paste the second exposure over the first. At this point it is essential to make sure the two images are in perfect register. Reduce the opacity of the upper layer to around 50-60%, select all of it and zoom into 100% or 200%. Select the Move Tool and move the upper image using the arrow keys, until it is in register with the background image,

OPACITIES

As used in Photoshop CS2 or earlier.

Layer position	Opacity
Layer 6	12%
Layer 5	17%
Layer 4	20%
Layer 3	25%
Layer 2	33%
Layer 1	50%
Background	100%

The original, shot in sequence at ISO 800.

then reset the opacity to 100%. Repeat this process for any other frames. With the images all in register, adjust the opacity of each to allow half of the image below to show through. This does not mean the same opacity setting for each, but instead a progressively lower opacity going up from the background. The table opposite shows the opacities.

In Photoshop CS3 (Extended), the process is more effective and easier, making use of the image stack Auto-Align features. First, copy and paste all the images into one layered image as above. An alternative is to load the layers with a script (*File > Scripts >* *Load Files into Stack*). Then select all the layers and run Auto-Align to put them into register. Convert the layers into a Smart Object and then choose a Stack Mode. The two useful modes for noise reduction are Median or Mean. Try both, but Median has the ability to replace pixels more drastically, rather than just reducing the strength of noisy pixels. Moreover, if there has been subject movement between frames, such as branches moving in wind, or a passer-by, Median can remove them. In any case, it is worth experimenting with both to see which is the more effective for a particular image.

PHOTOMATIX

One fast method of combining them is in Photomatix, using the Average choice. This automatically applies a median filter.

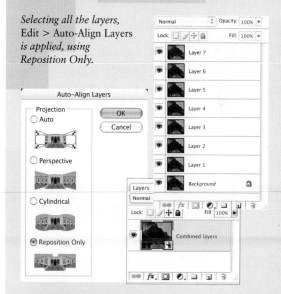

PHOTOSHOP

In Photoshop CS3 (extended edition only), the same combining procedure can be achieved too. It takes more steps, but is efficient. First copy all the frames into one image, as separate layers. Once the layers are merged into a Smart Object it's a simple matter of clicking *Layers > Smart Objects > Stack Mode > Median*.

Selecting all the layers, Edit > Auto-Align Layers is applied, using Reposition Only.

Original   *Photomatix*   *Photoshop CS3*

Result

Once aligned, the layer stack is converted into a Smart Object. This is achieved by highlighting all the layers and clicking Layer > Smart Objects > Convert to Smart Object.

MULTIPLE EXPOSURE CONTRAST

Locked down shooting makes it possible to take identical frames at successive exposures, for later combination into a single image by a variety of methods.

The high contrast caused by pooling of light (see page 10) is typical of many lowlight scenes, from a restaurant interior with spotlighting, to a city view at night. In the days of film this meant either bringing in photographic lighting to open up the shadows and balance the contrast, or simply accepting the high-contrast result with all its accompanying loss of detail. Now, however, this problem can be solved, particularly with a tripod. For subjects in which there is little or no movement, or at least where any movement is not a significant part of the image, the solution involves shooting the same scene at a number of different exposures, with no camera movement between frames.

As we'll see over the next 24 pages, there are a number of ways of combining a range of exposures, but the principle is always the same—to take the best detail from each individual exposure. So, with a high-contrast scene, the exposure that best deals with the middle range will likely overexpose highlights and underexpose shadows. Once the highlights have blown, at 255 on the histogram, the sensor photosites have essentially been flooded, and there is no detail captured at all. Correspondingly, serious underexposure renders deep shadows black (level 0), and while dark shadow areas may retain some detail that can be pulled up during processing by using Levels, Curves or a local-contrast process such as Photoshop's Shadows/Highlights feature, this will always be at the cost of increased noise. However, if in addition to the standard exposure that captures midtone detail, you shoot a longer exposure to capture shadows and a shorter exposure to capture highlights, you have effectively increased the amount of visual information you have to work with.

Another way of looking at this is that by bracketing exposures of the same scene, you are extending the dynamic range of the camera's sensor. Admittedly, this is not all in one frame, and the next steps on the

Traditional
The best of the traditionally exposed images has blown highlights around the lights and central window.

computer can be time-consuming and complex, but what is important is that you have captured much more detail than would otherwise have been possible. The bottom line is that if you have the time to do this, a range of exposures is a great back-up. You have lost nothing but a few megabytes of storage space, and gained a valuable archive of visual data. The following pages detail the current ways of handling this data, including the newest, HDRI, but we can also expect future imaging software to improve. The key lies in the capture.

The procedure is straightforward, but there are ways of making it more efficient and reliable. Clearly, the idea is not to move the camera at all between frames, and this makes a cable or remote release valuable, as well as good tripod use (making sure that it is firmly sited) and anything to reduce mirror slap, such as locking the mirror up. However, absolute precision to the pixel is not necessary. Desirable, certainly, but recent imaging software advances have made automatic alignment of images highly efficient to within several-to-many pixels. In

fact, this is one good example of what I just mentioned — future software advances. A few years ago, aligning different frames where there had been camera movement between them could be a painstaking manual task, particularly if an image layer needed rotation. Now, procedures such as Photoshop CS3's Auto-Align, and the similar features in most HDR generators (see page 196), bypass this completely.

One important alignment issue, however, is that you should vary the exposures by altering the shutter speed, not the aperture. Aperture affects depth of field, which can change the content of the image between frames, particularly as in low light you are likely not to be stopping down fully. There are two important considerations in working out how many frames and at what settings. The first is that the exposure gap between frames is short enough so that the software you use later for blending can be handle them, yet not so short that you clog up the memory card unnecessarily and take too long in shooting. As a rule of thumb,

HDR image
The result of merging several differently exposed frames shows more detail in areas that were completely blown in the example opposite.

181

MULTIPLE EXPOSURE CONTRAST

certainly for HDRI, 2 stops works well in most cases. One stop is safer, but usually redundant. Time and storage space are important, and many cameras have a small frame buffer, which can mean that you have to wait for frames to be processed by the camera before you can continuing shooting.

The second key consideration is to set the right limits for each end of the range. You need the shortest

SHOOTING THE SEQUENCE

First find (by measurement or trial and error) the shortest exposure which shows no highlight clipping. The most convenient indication is the flashing highlight warning. The shutter speed needed is the setting just shorter than this.

The first frame is the shortest shutter speed without clipping.

2 stops more.

2 stops more.

182

exposure to capture all significant highlight detail, and for this the best guide is the camera's on-screen flashing warning for highlight clipping. Nevertheless, you probably don't need every tonal detail of naked lamps. Treat these as you would specular highlights, and let them blow. This highlight clipping warning makes the shortest exposure the most convenient place to begin the sequence. From this, increase the exposures regularly between frames. Continue until the last exposure captures all the shadow detail that you want. Be warned that at night, because of the eye's adaptation and because the camera's LCD screen is likely to be much brighter than your surroundings, it's easy and normal to think that the exposures are brighter than they really are. As a precaution, and until you get used to doing this, continue at least one step beyond what you judge to be sufficient by eye. In addition, check the histogram display on the camera. For the last frame, capturing shadow detail, there should be a distinct peak on the right side. Failure to capture full shadow detail is the most common problem in shooting a range of exposures, and the penalty is noise.

The next frame is shot at 2 stops more exposure than this, using the shutter speed control only.

The next is 2 stops more again.

2 stops more.

The final exposure is the one that shows the darkest shadows at the midpoint in the histogram.

PROCEDURAL EXPOSURE BLENDING

This is arguably the earliest software system for combining differently exposed frames into one. The term "procedural," by the way, sets it apart from the manual brushing that we look at on the following pages. The principle is to place the different exposures in a stack of layers,

Although now a somewhat old-fashioned technique, two or three different exposures can be blended in Photoshop layers by making strong curve adjustments and applying different blending modes.

and then for each one select just the relevant detail. Thus, with the under-exposed frame that captures highlight detail but has blocked shadows, we need to adjust the curve and the blending mode so that only the highlight details are added to the combined result from this layer. Equally, with the over-exposed frame that captures shadow detail but has completely blown highlights, we need to isolate just the shadow areas.

The curve adjustments to do this need to be very strong; in fact, we need to drag one of the end points far away from the corner. Because this is non-intuitive, expect to make a number of trial-and-error adjustments. In the example here, the situation is about as simple as it can be—three exposures only, one for the highlights, another for the mid-range and a third for the shadows. The size of the exposure gap

between the three images determines the strength of the curve adjustment, and you will quickly appreciate the need for an exposure "overlap" between them. In other words, the over-exposed "shadow detail" frame needs to have some detail in the mid-range so that it will blend nicely with the middle layer.

The second part of the procedure is to blend the layers appropriately, using one of the many layer modes in Photoshop, as shown here. Typically, the images go from lightest (shadow details) at the bottom of the stack to darkest (highlight details) on top. Screen mode is used to add shadow detail, while Multiply mode is used to add highlight detail. So, with a three layer composite as in this example, you would first paste the midtone image over the light (shadow details) image, and set it (the upper layer) to Screen mode. Having adjusted the curve on the bottom layer to give the most realistic lightening of the shadows, paste the dark (highlight details) image on top of both, setting it to Multiply mode. Adjust the curve of the top layer to give the best-looking recovery of the highlights. Collapse the image. The result is likely to look a little flat, and will probably need an increase in contrast, by applying an S-curve in Curves, or by using the Midtone Contrast slider in the Shadows/Highlights control, or by applying the USM filter with a very large radius and small amount.

LOCKED DOWN

The original source images.

The midtone image is pasted over the lightest image, and its layer set to blend using the Screen blending mode.

The bottom (light) layer is selected, and an extreme curve applied which flattens contrast greatly but holds shadow details.

Next, the dark image is pasted on top of the other two, its blending mode set to Multiply, and left selected.

This dark image is given a different extreme curve, which also flattens contrast, but holds highlight detail.

To restore overall contrast, an S-curve is applied to the flattened image, heightening contrast in the midtones.

The Result.

Photomatix
For comparison, this is the blending result from Photomatix, using Highlight & Shadow Adjust.

MANUAL BLENDING

The least technical, most personal method of blending different exposures in a layer stack is to use the Eraser brush on an upper layer, so as to reveal better exposed detail underneath. In principle, nothing could be simpler, and it's worth saying that while Photoshop experts might treat such a non-procedural approach with some disdain, for photographic realism this is in no way an inferior technique. Indeed, with some types of image it can be more efficient too. Typically, the kinds of image that respond well to manual brushwork are those where the difference in exposure between the layers is confined to distinct spatial areas of the image. For instance, in a shot through a doorway or window from, say, a dark interior to a bright exterior, it may be fairly straightforward to select this hard-edged frame and then erase this part of an upper, light image layer.

Blending layers by brushwork gives a more personal control over the outcome; an artist's rather than a procedural approach.

Brush techniques tend to be idiosyncratic, in that most people simply develop their own particular ways. It is less valuable to try and categorize all of this than to show specific workthroughs. The examples here illustrate just some ways of doing this.

The original three source images, spaced 2 f stops apart.

The two darker images are pasted in as layers over the lightest, so that the layers are ordered darkest at the top, lightest at the bottom.

With the top, darkest layer turned off, erasing with a soft brush begins on the middle layer.

The middle layers is erased to leave just the exterior view.

Next, the top layer is made visible, and erased to leave all but the sunlit portions of the exterior.

The layer stack after the two upper images have been selectively erased by hand.

Final result, detail and whole image.

HIGH-LOW ISO BLENDING

A special technique for combining movement captured as high sensitivity with a clean, noise-free background

Consider a lowlight scene in which you have plenty of static fine detail that calls for a slow exposure that will be relatively noise-free, but at the same time there is some movement that you would also like to capture. The dilemma is whether to choose a low ISO setting and put up with motion blur in parts of the photograph, or a high ISO setting which will capture the movement, but increase the noise across everything. Remember from what we've seen of the different causes of noise that dark or fixed pattern noise is much easier to reduce than readout noise at a high ISO.

Well, there is a way of having the best of both worlds, although it takes more time, requires a tripod, and works successfully only in certain circumstances. The principle is to make two separate exposures, one at a low ISO and longer shutter speed, and the other with a high ISO and correspondingly short shutter speed. The two can then be combined later, choosing only the subject movement from the noisier high-ISO image. In effect, this drastically reduces the area over which you need to apply software noise reduction.

The example here illustrates the process and what it is capable of. In fact, I unintentionally made life more difficult for myself than it needed to be, because the first image was hand held at 1/20 sec and f4.2 at ISO 3200 and I did not have a tripod with me. Fortunately, my hotel was not too far away from this array of saké casks close to the Meiji Shrine in central Tokyo. I returned with the tripod and, using the LCD screen view of the image to help align the new shot, took the same view at ISO 100 and f11 at 4 sec. Returning like this obviously introduces some ethical questions about combining two images, but in my view this was acceptable on the grounds that, had I been energetic enough in the first place to be carrying and using a tripod, the two images would have been similar to any of the other multiple exposure techniques in this book. Be that as it may, the post-production involved running a noise-reducing filter over the figure of the old woman, combining this and the noise-free version in register as layers, and erasing the "noisy" background from around the figure. Reproduced small-scale as most of these pictures are here on these pages, the benefits are not so obvious, but practically this meant that the image could be printed acceptably up to exhibition size.

The Original
The original, hand-held shot, ISO 3200, as shot without noise correction.

Simple correction
The same, with noise correction applied using Noise Ninja (adjusted for best effect on the figure only).

Tripod shot
The second shot, taken at ISO 100, tripod-mounted.

The first image, processed in Noise Ninja for noise reduction, is pasted as a layer over the second, cleaner image.

At full scale to begin with, the surroundings are erased from the top layer using a large, soft brush.

Next, the eraser brush is reduced in size, and the erasing continued at magnification.

The final result.

Comparison
A detailed comparison of the key area of the image, where the figure and background are blended. From left to right: the first high-ISO noisy image, the same image processed for noise-reduction using Noise Ninja, the noise-reduced version combined with the second, noise-free image.

BLENDING SOFTWARE

LOCKED DOWN

Currently the most widely used dedicated software for blending a range of exposures is Photomatix, a cross-platform program that also handles HDR generation and tonemapping. Although both blending and hand tonemapping have a similar purpose in compressing a high dynamic range captured in different exposures), the techniques are quite different. Of the two, blending is simpler and easier to understand, and the several Photomatix options follow the same basic principle as the highlight-and-shadow blending method

Dedicated software aimed at combining different exposures gives a useful option that stops short of the more difficult HDRI.

described on page 118-119. They are, however, more refined and automated, and an obvious inexpensive choice if you plan to do this kind of shooting and combination on a regular basis.

Compare the description here with that of HDR and tonemapping on the following pages. Both methods use the same source files. Blending, which is called Exposure Blending in Photomatix terminology, selects highlight details from the less exposed images and shadows from the more fully exposed images. These are then combined in such a way that there is a smooth, unnoticeable transition across the midtones. The algorithms used make use of weighted averages, and in one of the five procedures offered this can be shifted by the user towards darker or lighter.

Originals
*The four original source images,
spaced 2 f stops apart.*

DIFFERENT PROCESSING

The algorithms for each are different, and as the results always need to be judged subjectively, as to how pleasing or otherwise they are to you, it is difficult to predict which to choose. Accordingly, Photomatix offer a batch-processing option, and recommend in case of any uncertainty using this to produce a range of results. You can then choose which looks best to you.

Average - This method combines images using the same averaging formula throughout the image, regardless of whether the computed pixels are in a dark or bright area. For this reason it cannot give the dynamic range extension possible with the other blending methods, but it has a natural effect and also has the effect of reducing noise

Highlights & Shadows - 2 Images This is the fastest procedure, and is optimized for exposures that are 3 to 4 stops apart. It can even produce a more satisfactory result from 2 images than another procedure using 3 or more source images.

Highlights & Shadows - Auto can handle more than two images, and is designed for a "natural looking" result. As a consequence, it errs on the side of flatness, with low contrast, but this can be improved later with any of the previously mentioned Photoshop contrast-enhancing techniques.

Highlights & Shadows - Adjust This gives you the choice of weighting the result towards the brighter or darker end of the range of source images, and also adjusting the radius (as this is a local-contrast enhancement method). A high radius produces a sharper-looking result, at the expense of a longer processing time, but runs the risk of halo artefacts around sharp changes in brightness.

Highlights & Shadows - Intensive This is intended to deal with a range of source images covering a very high dynamic range. There is a choice of two sub-procedures, Light or Enhanced, and the processing times for each is particularly long. With a high dynamic range, HDR and tonemapping is likely to be a better choice.

The Batch Processing window in Photomatix. For this exercise, the options have been selected. This is also a useful technique when there is uncertainty over which of the several blending methods will be best.

BLENDING SOFTWARE

Average

Adjust

Auto

Intensive (Light)

Intensive (Enhanced)

For comparison, an HDR file generated and tonemapping using the global operator (Tone Compressor).

Also for comparison, an HDR file generated and tonemapping using the local operator (Details Enhancer) at its default settings.

The HDR tonemapped in Details Enhancer with adjusted settings.

The tonemapped HDR further processed in Photoshop, using Shadows/Highlights to heighten mid-range contrast.

HDR IMAGING

When I first wrote about High Dynamic Range Imaging in 2005, it was used more in CGI (Computer Generated Imagery) for controlling lighting effects than in photography. Within a couple of years it was being used experimentally by a wide range of photographers eager to explore its ability to create hitherto impossible imagery. Predictably enough, it has been this strangeness that seems to have fueled its appeal to online picture-sharing communities.

Although difficult to use for a satisfactorily natural effect, and inherently unpredictable, High Dynamic Range Imaging has huge potential for getting closer to the way we see.

The more fundamental issues of how it matches perception and its relationship with naturalism, which were evident from the start, have still not been comprehensively addressed.

Seen from the perspective of how HDRI can be of service to photography rather than the other way around, there is still a way to go. This is still a relatively new technology and we can expect more progress in techniques and tools. Nevertheless, it is tailor-made for

several types of lowlight photography, including interiors with bright views out and bright city lighting. Both of these situations have huge dynamic ranges. I touched briefly on dynamic range on pages 20-21, but here it's important to distinguish between low and high. These are relative concepts, and for photography, it is the practical issue that decides. Essentially, if the dynamic range of the scene can be captured in a single exposure, with the possible exception of specular highlights, this is low.

Technically, therefore, 8 bits-per-channel is a low dynamic range format. 12-bit and 14-bit, which you can capture using Raw with a SLR, cover considerably more, but unfortunately most of the extra range is crowded into the highlights, where it is not really needed in photography, and little in the shadows, where it is. All camera sensors, therefore, work in a low dynamic range. In terms of scene lighting, this is usually adequate as long as there are no light sources in the frame, and as long as you do not need to pull out detail from visually deep shadows. Low lighting situations, however, often do feature lights in shot. An interior lit with only one desk lamp can cover 10 stops from close to the lamp to a dark shadow under the desk, while the lamp itself can extend this by 4 or 5 stops.

High Dynamic Range formats typically have 32 bits per channel, which alone expands the range hugely. However, the normal formats and color spaces, as well as the performance of monitor displays, use non-linear gamma encoding, and an important effect of this is that more of the bits are devoted to highlight information than to the shadow areas, as the diagram shows. In fact, the more bits per channel, the less efficiently the image is encoded digitally. To overcome this, HDR formats use their 32 bits per channel not as discrete allocations

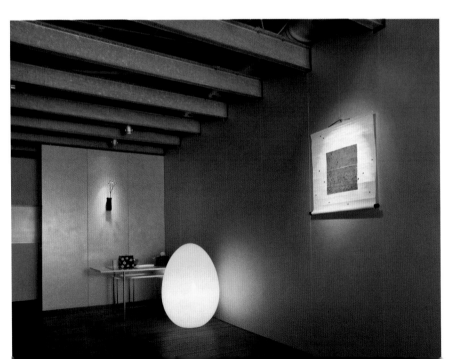

Light source in view
HDR and tonemapping easily meets the challenge of images in which the major light source is in view, as in this modern tea-ceremony room in Tokyo. Note also the holding of highlight detail in the spotlit wall-hanging.

of pixel values, but as decimal points. Floating point encoding assigns a precise value to every pixel, rather than forcing it into the nearest pre-determined level. The result is that an HDR file format can record a virtually infinite dynamic range, many millions to one.

An HDR format capable of recording these high ranges is one thing, but capturing is an-other. Currently there are only one or two specialized cameras that are capable of this, and for the rest of us the technique involves making a series of exposures at different shutter speeds. This makes HDR imaging practical only with the camera locked-down. In practice, 2 stops is the most convenient gap between exposures, and in order to avoid changing the structure of the image, it is better to alter the shutter speed than the aperture. A basic and effective way of shooting is to begin with an exposure which avoids clipped highlights, using trial and error and the camera's on-screen highlight warning. This is the shortest exposure of the series. Then lengthen the exposure time by 2 stops — 4 times the exposure, in other words — and take the second exposure. Keep doing this until the darkest shadows in the scene appear fully exposed; this looks like gross over-exposure on the LCD screen.

There are a number of software options for combining a series such as this into a single HDR image, and from the users point of view there is nothing complicated about it. The result is a 32 bits-per-channel floating point image that contains all the data from all of the exposures. It is, however, unviewable because nearly all monitors are 8-bit, and even the few with extended range are a modest 14-bit. The second part of the operation, therefore, involves compressing all of this data back down to 8 bits or 16 bits. There are a number of ways of doing this, but without any predictable best method. The essential difficulty is that the detailed execution of compressing a huge range into a small one depends on the nature of the image and on your interpretation of it. An HDR image has the potential to mimic human vision in its ability to take in a high dynamic range, but the eye and brain work quite differently. The subject is complex, but in perception the eyes scan in rapid, jerking movements known as saccades, and these multiple "recordings" are rapidly assembled in the brain into a coherent view. There is no way in principle of mimicking this in one flat image. The various stages of making an HDR image are covered in the following pages.

Church interior
Another classic HDR situation is the interior of a large church, or cathedral. HDR and tonemapping is able to open up deep shadow areas in the vaulting, while also rendering the much brighter stained glass windows accurately.

Photosphere
Although the situation will undoubtedly improve, browser and database support for 32-bit images is very limited. Photosphere is an exception — a fast browser that generates good previews on the fly from most standard HDR formats.

HDR GENERATION

Typically, the process of creating an HDR image begins with capture, which we dealt with on pages 180-183. The ease of creating an HDR file depends very much on this stage, because while the generation is largely automated, the software expects certain things from the captured sequence. It needs to access the exposure information, which is carried in the EXIF header, the exposures need to be appropriately spaced across the range, the several frames need to be in reasonably close alignment so that they can be matched, and for the same reason there should not be too much movement of objects within the scene. If all these conditions cannot be met there are ways of working around them, but with more difficulty.

An HDR generator is software that collates all the different exposure information from a sequence of exposures and then creates a single HDR image file. There are a number of generators available, some of them free, and while there are technical differences, for normal photography there is little to choose in performance. The most widely used are that supplied with Photoshop CS2 and CS3, and Photomatix. In use, all are relatively quick. Once the range of captured images has been selected, the generator looks for the exposure data in the EXIF headers.

Creating 32-bit-per-channel floating point images from a range of exposures is largely an automatic and trouble-free process, with a choice of formats.

HDR GENERATION IN PHOTOMATIX

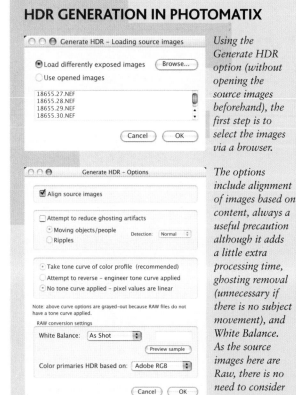

Using the Generate HDR option (without opening the source images beforehand), the first step is to select the images via a browser.

The options include alignment of images based on content, always a useful precaution although it adds a little extra processing time, ghosting removal (unnecessary if there is no subject movement), and White Balance. As the source images here are Raw, there is no need to consider a tone curve.

Once generated, the HDR image is previewed. The small preview windows show an on-the-fly view of small areas. In fact there is only one of these windows; three are shown here to illustrate the range that can be viewed in a few seconds by rolling the cursor over the image.

196

HDR GENERATION IN PHOTOSHOP

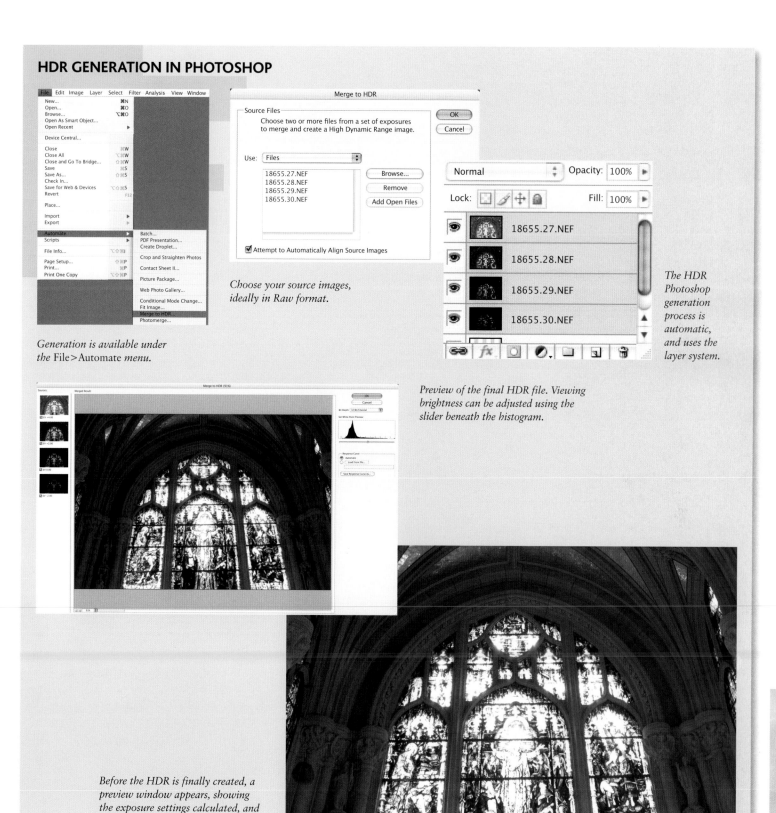

Generation is available under
the File>Automate menu.

Choose your source images,
ideally in Raw format.

The HDR
Photoshop
generation
process is
automatic,
and uses the
layer system.

Preview of the final HDR file. Viewing
brightness can be adjusted using the
slider beneath the histogram.

Before the HDR is finally created, a
preview window appears, showing
the exposure settings calculated, and
offering user adjustment of the white
point and the option to apply a
response curve.

HDR GENERATION

As both Photoshop and Photomatix can read Raw files, if you are shooting Raw there is no point whatsoever in first opening and adjusting the images with a Raw converter. All the information can be accessed directly by the HDR generator.

Once the 32-bit-per-channel HDR file has been created, it appears on screen as an extremely contrasty and sometimes dark image. A regular 8-bit monitor is no more able to display the full range of the image than an 8-bit file format is able to record all this exposure information. The viewing experience of an HDR file is predictably unsatisfactory, but to be practical there are few reasons for wanting to be able to look at the image at this stage, other than to check that nothing has gone seriously wrong, such as an image from another sequence wrongly added. Photoshop's solution for those who want to check details before moving on to tone-mapping (on the following pages) is a White Point Preview slider under the histogram that shows different parts of the range. This is especially useful for checking artifacts and sensor dust shadows.

Photomatix takes a different approach, adding a small viewer that reveals magnified detail under the cursor, and because the window covers only 177×134 pixels, the 8-bit view is usually intelligible. In practice, this happens in real time, so that moving the cursor across the image shows a rapidly shifting brightness, as shadows suddenly open up completely and highlights reveal full detail.

The final step in HDR generation is to save the image file in one of several formats, although many people choose to bypass this and go straight to tonemapping, in which case the HDR file is converted and lost. The two most commonly used formats are Radiance and OpenEXR. There are important differences between them, but more from the perspective of CGI and motion picture special effects, where accuracy across the entire range and file size (because of the huge number of frames in, say, an animated movie) matter. From a photographic perspective any of the available choices in the Save As dialog will do. If you plan to archive the HDR file, though, you may want to consider one of the more compact formats, such as OpenEXR.

FILE SIZES

This table shows the relative file sizes of an image of identical pixel dimensions when saved using different HDR file formats. All of the top three formats offer 76 orders of magnitude dynamic range, but TIFF LogLuv32 manages "only" 38.

File Format	Encoding	File Size (MB)
Radiance	RGBE	3
Radiance	XYZE	3
TIFF	IEEE RGB	10
TIFF	LogLuv32	2.4

HDR GENERATION IN FDRTOOLS

Generic DCRAW (*.crw;*.cr2;*.dcr;*.dng;*.mrw;*.nef;*.orf;*.pef;*.raf;*.srf;*.sr2)
Generic JPEG (*.jpg;*.jpeg)
✓ Generic TIFF (*.tif;*.tiff)
Generic RGBE (*.hdr;*.rgbe)
Generic OpenEXR (*.exr)

All Documents

The selection process through a browser window requires the file type to be chosen first.

The selected files appear in a window that allows manual readjustment of alignment, at the same time as a large preview window. Note that this preview can be switched to a default tonemapped preview. Generation in FDRTools is unusual in that it is retained as part of the entire tonemapping procedure. Source images can even be deselected.

Switching to the Separation option shows which parts of which image's tonal ranges are being used—and these can be altered manually. The default is usually good.

TONEMAPPING

The crucial and most difficult step in High Dynamic Range Imaging is mapping the extreme range of tones down to 8-bits or 16-bits per channel.

The final stage in HDR Imaging is to create a viewable 16-bit or 8-bit image from the 32-bit HDR file. This is neither predictable nor particularly easy to manage, although there are several software methods. Much depends on the original scene, how big a dynamic range it has, and the way you shot it, but for various reasons simply compressing it to fit a 256-level scale is rarely satisfactory. If there are very bright highlights, for example, a simple proportionate compression will result in an overall dark image with insufficient attention paid to the midtones. Because the many tones in the HDR file have to be assigned somehow to the much more restricted low dynamic range (LDR) file, the procedure is called tonemapping. The software that performs this operation is known as a tonemapping operator, sometimes referred to by the shorthand TMO. The several tonemapping operators available are the result of various ingenious algorithms that attempt to give a result that is a compromise between retaining tonal detail across the scale and looking realistic. This last, realism, is the biggest problem in tonemapping, because it represents a cross over between the subjective and the psychology of perception.

All of this means that in practice there is a considerable amount of trial and error, and you may often want to try out more than one operator to see which looks best for you in which situation. There are two classes of tonemapping operator (TMO); global and local. A global operator works on the entire range of tonal values in much the same way, as does, for example, a tone curve on any image (think of normal Curves or Levels operations in Photoshop). Global operators have the advantage of giving results that look photographically normal, therefore realistic, but they have the disadvantage of usually sacrificing detail and contrast in some areas of the image. A common example of a global operator is a pair of sliders controlling gamma and exposure. Playing with both will usually produce an image that is acceptable but often flat.

The second class of TMO is the local operator. These algorithms, which vary considerably in the principles on which they work, adjust the tonal value of each pixel according to its neighbors. This makes it possible to adjust local contrast, and potentially this is a very powerful way of mapping tonal values. Accordingly, one of the key adjustments here is the radius — the distance around each pixel that is searched. If you are already familiar and comfortable with other radius-based procedures, particularly unsharp masking and Shadows/Highlights in Photoshop, you will become accustomed to these local operators more easily. The advantage of a local operator is that it can handle even wide dynamic ranges with surprising efficiency. The disadvantages are that the results can often look false and over-detailed, there is a danger of halos around distinct areas (such as the sky close to a window frame or a horizon), the results are difficult to predict and the user settings are non-intuitive. Local operators need considerable assistance from various controls.

Full size HDR
HDR tonemapping makes it possible to shoot in very contrasty lighting, such as in a bar and restaurant without special lighting, and still achieve an attractive and controlled result.

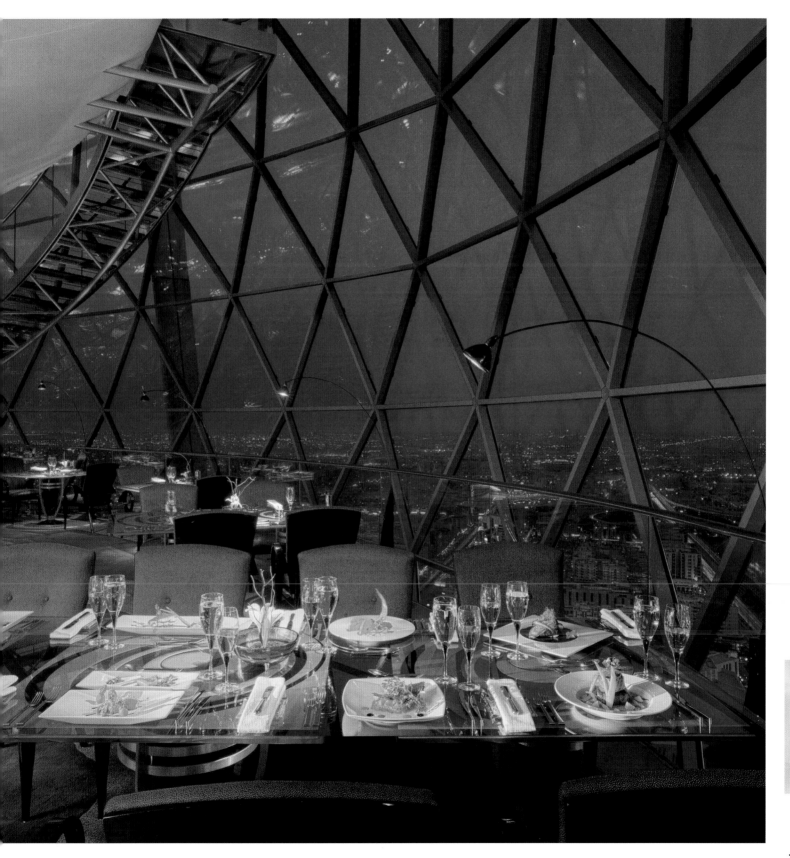

TONEMAPPING

In both cases, global and local, it is normal for the image to need further work. Getting the tonemapping right in one go is difficult, often impossible. Local operators in particular are likely to look rather flat. For this reason, it is essential to produce from a 16-bit image the HDR 32-bit file. After further adjustment, which would otherwise lose data and result in a spiky, toothcomb-like histogram, you can then reduce it to a final 8-bit image. The most usual post-procedures for tweaking a 16-bit file are Curves or Levels, Shadows/ Highlights. and even the mild local contrast enhancement of USM used with a large radius and small amount (as described on page 211).

Color saturation is another issue. Basically, the more extreme the gradient of tonal mapping, the more saturated the final color is likely to be, and this often results in certain colors appearing far too rich. Some local operators have a color saturation control, but in any case, you can expect to need to perform some adjustment on the output 16-bit image. The Hue/ Saturation sliders are an obvious choice, but a more targeted procedure is the Replace Color tool in Photoshop's *Image>Adjustment* menu.

Tonemapping is, above all, very specific. HDR software designed for photographers began with Photomatix, was followed by Photoshop, and now includes a few more, notably FDRTools and easyHDR. There will undoubtedly be more to come. Each works in a particular way, different from the others.

Processed comparison
In the processed comparison, the best original frame (LDR, low dynamic range) is on the left; in the centre is the HDR global tonemapped version and on the right the locally tonemapped version, both in Photomatix. Global tonemapping does a satisfactory and realistic job of combing the exposures, but comes nowhere near the local tonemapping operator, which holds detail in each tonal neighborhood of pixels, from highlight to shadow.

Chromatic aberration

Lateral chromatic aberration is exaggerated strongly in the process of generating and tonemapping an HDR. This small detail from the corner of an image, uncorrected and corrected, gives an idea of the extent of this problem.

Originals

Enlargements of a detail — one of the spotlit dishes from the restaurant image on page 201 — shows the original sequence of 5 frames, each separated by the standard 2 f stops.

PHOTOMATIX

Photomatix is the pioneer HDR application for photography (as has already been noted, HDR has other uses, notably in computer-generated imaging), and in the current crop of available software is noted for the large number of user controls that it offers. One result of this is that it enables a wide range of possible treatments for any image, including some highly non-realistic ones.

Photomatix offers a basic choice between Tone Compressor (its global operator) and Details Enhancer (its local operator).

Photomatix is a powerful tool that offers more controls than most of its competitors.

As with other HDR software, the global operator sticks close to "photographic" realism, but is much less effective in tonemapping, so that with a wide range of exposures in the original sequence, the local operator — Details Enhancer — is the usual choice. The default setting is designed to give a reasonable and realistic result under most circumstances, and it is best to begin with this. A powerful and unique feature of Photomatix is its choice of five Luminosity settings, which allows you much greater control over the resulting HDR image than other software does.

HDR Preview
The HDR preview, prior to tonemapping. The useful small preview window shows detail under the cursor.

The default settings are reasonable, but the overall effect is too light and lacking in mid-tone contrast. The Light Smoothing setting is appropriate for this image.

There is probably too much opening up of local tones, as the dynamic range of the image is only medium-high, so the Strength is reduced. Then, to increase contrast, the Luminosity and Gamma sliders are moved in opposition (Luminosity to the right, Gamma to the left, which is to say, both raised).

Microcontrast is raised to enhance small-scale detailed contrast in the grain of the doors, accompanied by a slight increase in Micro-smoothing to avoid harshness.

Photomatix to Photoshop
The image is saved in 16-bit and opened in Photoshop for further post-processing. Typical of HDR tonemapping is the too-dark rendering of white walls when there are other, brighter whites in the image. There is no completely satisfactory way of dealing with this in the tonemapping process. Note also the subtle differences between the tonemapping preview and the result on the full-sized image.

Shadows and Highlights
The first Photoshop correction is a lightening of the white walls, accompanied by an increase in mid-tone contrast, using the Shadows/Highlights tool.

Blue doors
The reflection of the window in the surface of the doors is distracting and too blue (because of the higher color temperature). Replace Color is used to lower the saturation and brightness of a selected area by careful adjustment of the Fuzziness (radius) slider.

Softening yellow
The particular shade of orange-yellow above the doors in the mezzanine bedroom, caused by CFL (Compact Fluorescent Lighting) is not attractive. Replace Color is used a second time to make a slight hue shift, desaturation and lightening of this area.

The final result

PHOTOSHOP

T he Photoshop tonemapping procedure is initiated simply by changing Mode from 32-bit to 16-bit or 8-bit. Once you select either of these two, the dialog window offers four ways of tone-mapping, of which the first three are generally of little use. The very first is Exposure/Gamma, a straightforward pairing of an exposure slider (for brightness) and a gamma slider (for contrast combined with brightness), which offers very basic global tonemapping. The second is Highlight Compression, which applies a custom tonal curve to reduce highlight contrast drastically so as to brighten the rest of the image and restore contrast. The third is Equalize Histogram, which applies a

Photoshop's tonemapping tool offers a variety of options

different custom tonal curve to even out peaks in the histogram. All of these are global operators.

The fourth and most generally useful is Local Adaptation. The main control is a curve superimposed on a histogram, making this one of the most intuitive operators. As this is selected, in default and without adjustment, the image is most likely to appear quite strange. As most photographs, even of very contrasty scenes, are likely to occupy only the central part of the scale, the result will often be very bright and with strong, unrealistic colors. The first step is to close the curve to approximately the dark and light limits of the image as shown by the histogram. One method is to drag the end-points of the curve, another is to click on the curve in two positions, high and low, and then check the Corner tick box. This has the effect of

Starting the process
Changing Mode from 32-bit to either 16-bit or 8-bit initiates the process. 16-bit conversion is recommended if any further post-processing is likely (as it usually is after tonemapping).

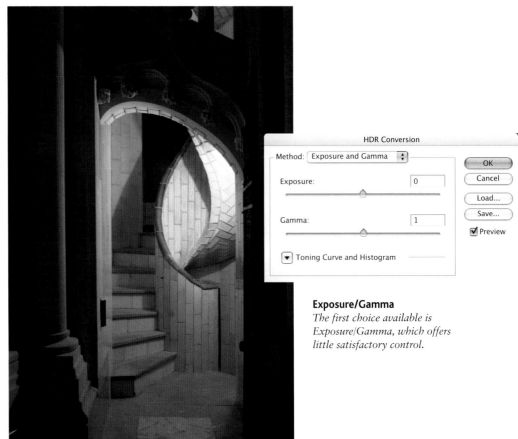

Exposure/Gamma
The first choice available is Exposure/Gamma, which offers little satisfactory control.

isolating the central section of the curve. Drag the lower control point until it is just over the darkest point of the histogram; this will immediately make the image preview look more realistic. For the time being leave the high point where it is, making sure only that it is vertically positioned over the highest part of the histogram. Then adjust the central section of the curve for appearance. The position of the upper control point, which is basically holding the bright highlights, can then be judged. Lowering it darkens the highlights, which can create a flat falseness, while raising it brightens them, which can lose information at the expense of a more photographic look.

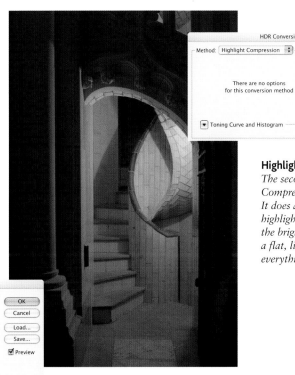

Highlight compression
The second option, Highlight Compression, is not adjustable. It does a good job of preserving highlight detail, visible in the brightest tiles, but gives a flat, lifeless rendering of everything else.

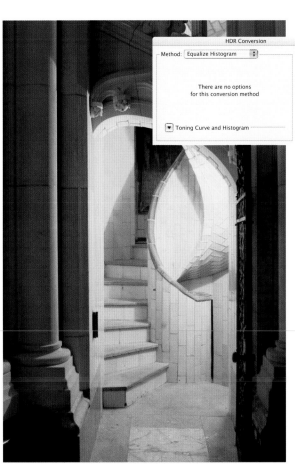

Equalize histogram
The third option, Equalize Histogram, is also not adjustable. It does a reasonable job on mid-to-dark tones, but fails to hold highlight detail.

Local adaptation
Local Adaptation allows much more control. Here, using the default radius and threshold, the curve has been "divided" into four sections by "corners" or knee-points, allowing dark shadows and bright highlights to be maintained, while working separately on two tonal ranges. The lower mid-tones are lightened slightly, and the higher mid-tones have been given a contrast-enhancing S-curve.

FDR TOOLS

A relative newcomer is this piece of cross-platform software which hails from Germany. It has two especially notable features. One is the integration of creating HDR files from the source images with tonemapping, the other is the deliberate simplification of the controls aimed at producing realistic results in a few steps. We already saw something of the HDR generation on pages 196-199, but whereas in other software this is a separate operation from tonemapping, with FDRTools it is combined with the tonemapping in the sense that at any point during tonemapping you can return to the HDR creation and make a number of adjustments. These include choosing

FDRTools, or Full Dynamic Range Tools, provides an exceptionally clean and easy-to-use interface.

which tonal ranges are used from which source images, tweaking the choice of images to use for ghosting removal, or even opting to drop one or more of the images (see pages 214-215).

The three principle controls in the local operator (called Compressor), are Compression, Contrast and Smoothing. Compression controls the strength, more on local contrast than on global, and a higher setting is needed for HDR files with a high dynamic range. Too high, however, tends to flatten the general appearance, and adds a veiling fog across strong luminosity edges. The Contrast slider affects large-scale and mid-scale contrast, and is complementary to Compression. Increasing its strength improves overall contrast. The Smoothing slider does what it says — it smooths the potentially harsh effects of high values in the other two slider.

Default options

The opening default windows. Compressor, selected here, is FDRTools' name for the local operator (the opposite of the terms used by Photomatix). There are three user sliders, Compression, Contrast, and Smoothing. The main image window (Navigator) shows the effect, with the usual limitation that the final results are affected by scale. A Preview window gives a 100% view, and can be sized and repositioned at will like other windows of your desktop.

208

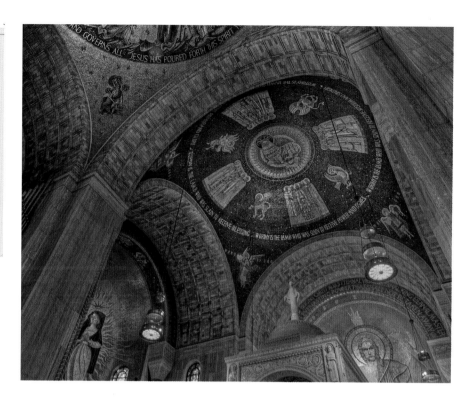

The result from the first stage

Experimenting with the options

With only three user parameters, experimenting with different tonemapping options is relatively fast and simple. The settings finally chosen for this moderately high contrast image were high in all three. The gamma was reduced just a touch to optimize the brightness.

Opening the saved image in Photoshop (FDRTools provides this option), it was felt that the result needed some brightening in the midtones and more contrast in the lower midtones. The curve created in the Curves dialog achieves this by holding down the highlights and the deep shadows.

A low amount/high radius unsharp mask adds extra punch, a form of midtone contrast increase.

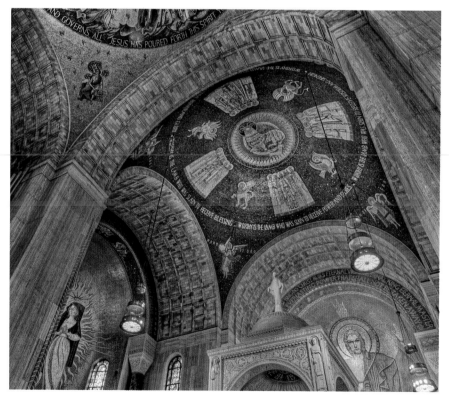

The final result

EASY HDR

A nother relative newcomer is this software (available for Microsoft Windows only); indeed it has only been available since 2006 when it emerged with the specific aim of facilitating astrophotography like a shot of the moon with shining aureole. It now aims to achieve realistic rather than artificial and over-dramatic results in all HDR situations. In terms of the number of user controls offered, it falls somewhere between Photomatix and FDRTools. Its most powerful features are in a local operator, which has strength, brightness, smoothness, and edge sub-options. It combines this with a global operator that can also be used to post-process the locally tonemapped image within the application. The global operator is always active (and intended for post-processing), but checking the Mask option enables the local operator. They both appear in this workthrough, and the resulting file is a standard 8-bit or 16-bit TIFF.

EasyHDR offers a tailored toolset that aims for realistic rather than artificial results.

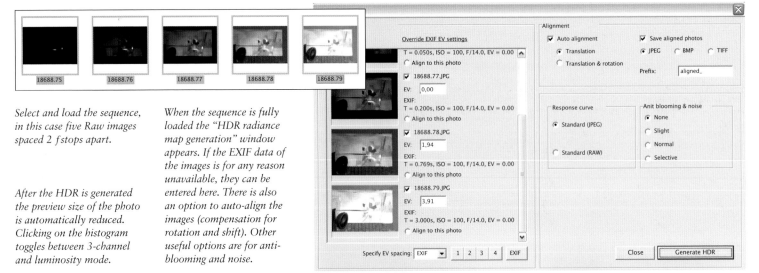

Select and load the sequence, in this case five Raw images spaced 2 f stops apart.

After the HDR is generated the preview size of the photo is automatically reduced. Clicking on the histogram toggles between 3-channel and luminosity mode.

When the sequence is fully loaded the "HDR radiance map generation" window appears. If the EXIF data of the images is for any reason unavailable, they can be entered here. There is also an option to auto-align the images (compensation for rotation and shift). Other useful options are for anti-blooming and noise.

The histogram shows that most of the image pixels have low luminosity relative to the maximum value. The curves tool allows the

histogram to be stretched in order to better use the available dynamic range.

FAR LEFT: The smoothness for the tone mapping mask is increased to match the image size (which is ten megapixels).

LEFT: The tone mapping mask is tuned, using both "Strength" and "Brightness" settings to brighten shadows and attenuate the bright areas.

RIGHT: The Compression slider is increased in order to get good contrast while reducing the dynamic range.

The gamma value is adjusted to lower the brightness. It is also possible to trim the histogram in order to increase contrast while losing only a couple of pixels by clipping them to white or black. Checking the "Mark overexposed and underexposed areas" checkbox shows which areas are overexposed or underexposed.

The "Process all" button is clicked to process the whole image at full resolution. Post-processing is also possible at this stage.

The image is finally rotated and saved as a 16-bit per channel TIFF.

GHOSTING

Ghosting is the term given to superimposed, displaced parts of an image, quite common in any multiple-exposure technique when parts of the subject move. If you are shooting a scene with passers-by, for example, then it is inevitable that they will be in different positions in each of the frames. Moreover, as this is low light photography, some or all of the frames are likely to show a degree of motion blurring.

A problem with all multiple-exposure techniques is how to deal with subjects that move positions because of the lag between frames.

Many HDR generators, however, have some provision for attempting to remove ghosting. This works typically by detecting the variance in the image — the areas where the content differs — and then by giving priority to one frame of the sequence. This works most successfully when there are very few frames and movement in just one or two frames, as in the example here. Varied movement across a large number of frames, and in which the movement overlaps, can cause problems. It also helps when the movement is in an area with a similar tonal range, as movement across a strong luminosity edge, such as a skyline, can also cause failure. FDRTools notably allows adjustment of exactly how the frames are prioritized for ghosting removal, a useful option.

Finally, consider using the high-low ISO blending technique described on page 188. In this case you can

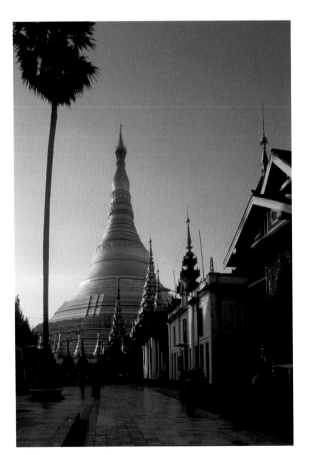

First frame
The first frame, exposed for the sky and highlights on the pagoda.

Second frame
Less than a minute later, the second frame, exposed for the shadow areas in the fore-ground, where the three people are walking.

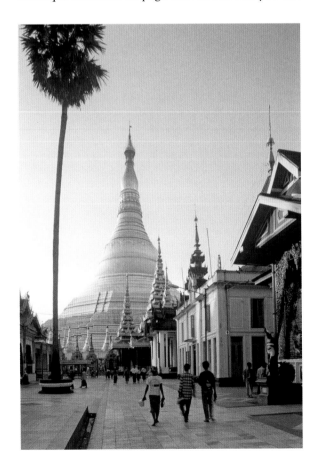

expect tonal differences, but as the purpose is to select just moving subjects, such as people, this should not normally cause too many problems. When shooting, take one or a few frames at a sufficiently high ISO to allow a reasonably short shutter speed. The frame should in any case be in register with the HDR image. Paste on top after the HDR image has been tone-mapped to 16-bit, check that it is in register by clicking this upper layer on and off quickly, and if any repositioning is necessary, do this now with the arrow keys. Next, erase around the objects that you want to keep, to replace their ghosted versions in the tone-mapped HDR image, then adjust the tone and color to match, using Curves or Levels. Finally you will need to flatten the image.

Illustrated on this spread is an extremely simple situation for ghosting, with just two differently exposed frames, and so hardly HDR, but it illustrates the technique well. The two images were used to generate an HDR file in Photomatix, with ghost removal activated. For comparison, the result without ghost removal simply appears as a double exposure.

Detail comparison
In close-up, the area with the variance. On the left, without ghosting removal during HDR generation, on the right, with.

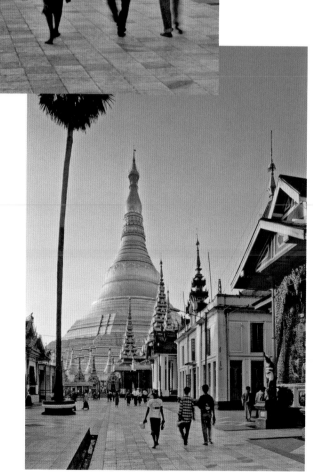

Standard combination
Combining the two images as a 32-bit-per-channel HDR image in Photomatix and then tonemapping. The blending of the two images without the option of removing ghosting has the predictable result of a 50% blend across the movement.

Ghosting removal
Choosing the ghosting removal option during the HDR generation step prioritizes the second frame for the foreground.

GLOSSARY

Computing is awash with jargon. No, worse than that—it *breeds* jargon, making a large part of most computer magazines, for example, unintelligible to any but the initiated. Similarly photography and the assortment of associated arts (of which lighting is just one), is a world which can shield itself from outsiders in a protective cloak of terminology. Merge the two, as we must for this book, and life can become complicated for even the most patient of readers. On top of that, and especially in the area of lighting terminology, there are always crossovers in meaning; a "flag" and a "gobo" (go between) can mean the same thing to one photographer and be separate entities to another, for example.

Despite rigorous attempts at editing, I realize that this book still uses a fairly full complement of jargon, and to be honest, removing any more than I already have would not help. If you find some of the computer terms especially difficult, you might like to try this book's sister title, *The Complete Guide to Digital Photography (ISBN 1-57990-759-8)* for a more gentle learning curve. Here, though, I've attempted to compile all the terms that may be unfamiliar when you first open the book. Explaining concepts in many words every time would simply become irritating to read, as well as to write. I'm afraid that we're stuck with much of this jargon. The best solution seems to me to have a substantial glossary to cope with it.

aperture The opening behind the camera lens through which light passes on its way to the image sensor (CCD/CMOS).

artifact A flaw in a digital image.

axis lighting Light aimed at the subject from close to the camera's lens.

backlighting The result of shooting with a light source, natural or artificial, behind the subject to create a silhouette or rim-lighting effect.

ballast The power pack unit for an HMI light which provides a high initial voltage.

barn doors The adjustable flaps on studio lighting equipment which can be used to control the beam emitted.

barn door tracker A remarkably effective device used by amateur photographers to turn a camera to follow the movement of stars across the night sky.

bit (binary digit) The smallest data unit of binary computing, being a single 1 or 0.

bit depth The number of bits of color data for each pixel in a digital image. A photographic-quality image needs eight bits for each of the red, green, and blue channels, making for a bit depth of 24.

boom A support arm for attaching lights or fittings to.

bracketing A method of ensuring a correctly exposed photograph by taking three shots; one with the supposed correct exposure, one slightly underexposed, and one slightly overexposed.

brightness The level of light intensity. One of the three dimensions of color in the HSB color system. See also Hue and Saturation

byte Eight bits. The basic unit of desktop computing. 1,024 bytes equals one kilobyte (KB), 1,024 kilobytes equals one megabyte (MB), and 1,024 megabytes equals one gigabyte (GB).

calibration The process of adjusting a device, such as a monitor, so that it works consistently with others, such as scanners or printers.

candela Measure of the brightness of a light source itself.

CCD (Charge-Coupled Device) A tiny photocell used to convert light into an electronic signal. Used in densely packed arrays, CCDs are the recording medium in most digital cameras.

channel Part of an image as stored in the computer; similar to a layer. Commonly, a color image will have a channel allocated to each primary color (e.g. RGB) and sometimes one or more for a mask or other effects.

cloning In an image-editing program, the process of duplicating pixels from one part of an image to another.

CMOS (Complementary Metal-Oxide Semiconductor) An alternative sensor technology to the CCD, CMOS chips are used in ultra-high-resolution cameras from Canon and Kodak.

CMYK (Cyan, Magenta, Yellow, Key) The four process colors used for printing, including black (key).

color gamut The range of color that can be produced by an output device, such as a printer, a monitor, or a film recorder.

color temperature A way of describing the color differences in light, measured in Kelvins and using a scale that ranges from dull red (1900 K), through orange, to yellow, white, and blue (10,000 K).

compression Technique for reducing the amount of space

that a file occupies, by removing redundant data. There are two kinds of compression: standard and lossy. While the first simply uses different, more processor-intensive routines to store data than the standard file formats (see LZW), the latter actually discards some data from the image. The best known lossy compression system is JPEG, which allows the user to choose how much data is lost as the file is saved.

contrast The range of tones across an image, from bright highlights to dark shadows.

cropping The process of removing unwanted areas of an image, leaving behind the most significant elements.

depth of field The distance in front of and behind the point of focus in a photograph, in which the scene remains in acceptable sharp focus.

dialog box An onscreen window, part of a program, for entering settings to complete a procedure.

diffusion The scattering of light by a material, resulting in a softening of the light and of any shadows cast. Diffusion occurs in nature through mist and cloud cover, and can also be simulated using diffusion sheets and soft-boxes.

digital zoom Many cheaper cameras offer a digital zoom function. This simply crops from the center of the image and scales the image up using image processing algorithms (indeed the same effect can be achieved in an image editor later). Unlike a zoom lens, or "optical zoom," the effective resolution is reduced as the zoom level increases; 2× digital zoom uses ¼ of the image sensor area, 3× uses ⅑, and so on. The effect of this is very poor image quality; Even if you start with an eight megapixel sensor,

at just 3× digital zoom your image would be taken from less than one megapixel of it.

DMax (Maximum Density) The maximum density—that is, the darkest tone—that can be recorded by a device.

DMin (Minimum Density) The minimum density—that is, the brightest tone—that can be recorded by a device.

dye sublimation printer A color printer that works by transferring dye images to a substrate (paper, card, etc.) by heat, to give near photographic-quality prints.

edge lighting Light that hits the subject from behind and slightly to one side, creating flare or a bright "rim lighting" effect around the edges of the subject.

feathering In image-editing, the fading of the edge of an image or selection.

file format The method of writing and storing information (such as an image) in digital form. Formats commonly used for photographs include TIFF, BMP, and JPEG.

fill-in flash A technique that uses the on-camera flash or an external flash in combination with natural or ambient light to reveal detail in the scene and reduce shadows.

fill light An additional light used to supplement the main light source. Fill can be provided by a separate unit or a reflector.

filter (1) A thin sheet of transparent material placed over a camera lens or light source to modify the quality or color of the light passing through. (2) A feature in an image-editing application that alters or transforms selected pixels for some kind of visual effect.

flag Something used to partially block a light source to control the amount of light that falls on the subject.

flash meter A light meter especially designed to verify exposure in flash photography. It does this by recording values from the moment of a test flash, rather than simply measuring the "live" light level.

focal length The distance between the optical center of a lens and its point of focus when the lens is focused on infinity.

focal range The range over which a camera or lens is able to focus on a subject (for example, 0.5m to Infinity).

focus The optical state where the light rays converge on the film or CCD to produce the sharpest possible image.

fringe In image-editing, an unwanted border effect to a selection, where the pixels combine some of the colors inside the selection and some from the background.

frontal light Light that hits the subject from behind the camera, creating bright, high-contrast images, but with flat shadows and less relief.

f-stop The calibration of the aperture size of a photographic lens.

gamma A measure of the contrast of an image, expressed as the steepness of the characteristic curve of an image.

gobo A corruption of "go between," this is anything used to block or partially block light.

gradation The smooth blending of one tone or color into another, or from transparent to colored in a tint. A graduated lens filter, for

instance, might be dark on one side, fading to clear on the other.

grayscale An image made up of a sequential series of 256 gray tones, covering the entire gamut between black and white.

halogen bulb Common in modern spotlighting, halogen lights use a tungsten fillament surrounded by halogen gas, allowing it to burn hotter, longer and brighter.

haze The scattering of light by particles in the atmosphere, usually caused by fine dust, high humidity, or pollution. Haze makes a scene paler with distance, and softens the hard edges of sunlight.

HDRI (High Dynamic Range Imaging) A method of combining digital images taken at different exposures to draw detail from areas which would traditionally have been over or under exposed. This effect is typically achieved using a Photoshop plugin, and HDRI images can contain significantly more information than can be rendered on screen or even percieved by the human eye.

histogram A map of the distribution of tones in an image, arranged as a graph. The horizontal axis goes from the darkest tones to the lightest, while the vertical axis shows the number of pixels in that range.

HMI (Hydrargyrum Medium-arc Iodide) A lighting technology known as "daylight" since it provides light with a color temperature of around 5600 K.

honeycomb grid In lighting, a grid can be placed over a light to prevent light straying. The light can either travel through the grid in the correct direction, or will be absorbed by the walls of each cell in the honeycomb.

hot-shoe An accessory fitting found on most digital and film SLR cameras and some high-end compact models, normally used to control an external flash unit. Depending on the model of camera, pass information to lighting attachments via the metal contacts of the shoe.

HSB (Hue, Saturation, Brightness) The three dimensions of color, and the standard color model used to adjust color in many image-editing applications.

hue The pure color defined by position on the color spectrum; what is generally meant by "color" in lay terms.

incandescent lighting This strictly means light created by burning, referring to traditional filament bulbs. They are also know as hotlights, since they remain on and become very hot.

incident meter A light meter as opposed to the metering systems built into many cameras. These are used by hand to measure the light falling at a paticular place, rather than (as the camera does) the light reflected from a subject.

ISO An international standard rating for film speed, with the film getting faster as the rating increases. ISO 400 film is twice as fast as ISO 200, and will produce a correct exposure with less light and/or a shorter exposure. However, higher-speed film tends to produce more grain in the exposure, too.

Joule Measure of power, see watt-seconds.

JPEG (Joint Photographic Experts Group) Pronounced "jay-peg," a system for compressing images, developed as an industry standard by the International Standards Organization. Compression ratios are typically between 10:1 and 20:1, although

lossy (but not necessarily noticeable to the eye).

kelvin Scientific measure of temperature based on absolute zero (simply take 273.15 from any temperature in Celsius to convert to kelvin). In photography measurements in kelvin refer to color temperature. Unlike other measures of temperature, the degrees symbol in not used.

lasso In image-editing, a tool used to draw an outline around an area of an image for the purposes of selection.

layer In image-editing, one level of an image file, separate from the rest, allowing different elements to be edited separately.

LCD (Liquid Crystal Display) Flat screen display used in digital cameras and some monitors. A liquid-crystal solution held between two clear polarizing sheets is subject to an electrical current, which alters the alignment of the crystals so that they either pass or block the light.

light pipe A clear plastic material that transmits like, like a prism or optical fiber.

light tent A tent-like structure, varying in size and material, used to diffuse light over a wider area for close-up shots.

lumens A measure of the light emitted by a lightsource, derived from candela.

luminaires A complete light unit, comprising an internal focussing mechanism and a fresnel lens. An example would be a focusing spot light. The name luminaires derives from the French, but is used by professional photographers across the world.

luminosity The brightness of a color, independent of the hue or saturation.

lux A scale for measuring illumination, derived from lumens. It is defined as one lumen per square meter, or the amount of light falling from a light source of one candela one meter from the subject.

LZW (Lempel-Ziv-Welch) A standard option when saving TIFF files which reduces file sizes, especially in images with large areas of similar color. This option does not lose any data from the image, but cannot be opened by some image editing programs.

macro A mode offered by some lenses and cameras that enables the lens or camera to focus in extreme close-up.

mask In image-editing, a grayscale template that hides part of an image. One of the most important tools in editing an image, it is used to limit changes to a particular area or protect part of an image from alteration.

megapixel A rating of resolution for a digital camera, directly related to the number of pixels forming or output by the CMOS or CCD sensor. The higher the megapixel rating, the higher the resolution of images created by the camera.

midtone The parts of an image that are approximately average in tone, falling midway between the highlights and shadows.

modelling light A small light built into studio flash units which remains on continiously. It can be used to position the flash, approximating the light that will be cast by the flash.

monobloc An all-in-one flash unit with the controls and power supply built-in. Monoblocs can be synchronized together to create more elaborate lighting setups.

noise Random pattern of small spots on a digital image that are generally unwanted, caused by nonimage-forming electrical signals.

open flash The technique of leaving the shutter open and triggering the flash one or more times, perhaps from different positions in the scene.

peripheral An additional hardware device connected to and operated by the computer, such as a drive or printer.

pixel (PICture ELement) The smallest units of a digital image, pixels are the square screen dots that make up a bitmapped picture. Each pixel carries a specific tone and color.

photoflood bulb A special tungsten light, usually in a reflective dish, which produces an especially bright (and if suitably coated white) light. The bulbs have a limited lifetime.

plug-in In image-editing, software produced by a third party and intended to supplement a program's features or performance.

power pack The separate unit in flash lighting systems (other than monoblocks) which provides power to the lights.

ppi (pixels-per-inch) A measure of resolution for a bitmapped image.

processor A silicon chip containing millions of micro-switches, designed for performing specific functions in a computer or digital camera.

QuickTime VR An Apple-developed technology that allows a series of photos to be joined in a single file which the user can then use to look around, say, a product or a room.

RAID (Redundant Array of Independent Disks) A stack of hard disks that function as one, but with greater capacity.

RAM (Random Access Memory) The working memory of a computer, to which the central processing unit (cpu) has direct, immediate access.

raw files A digital image format, known sometimes as the "digital negative," which preserves higher levels of color depth than traditional 8 bits per channel images. The image can then be adjusted in software—potentially by three *f* stops—without loss of quality. The file also stores camera data including meter readings, aperture settings and more. In fact each camera model creates its own kind of raw file, though leading models are supported by software like Adobe Photoshop.

reflector An object or material used to bounce available light or studio lighting onto the subject, often softening and dispersing the light for a more attractive end result.

resampling Changing the resolution of an image either by removing pixels (lowering resolution) or adding them by interpolation (increasing resolution).

resolution The level of detail in a digital image, measured in pixels (e.g. 1,024 by 768 pixels), or dots-per-inch (in a half-tone image, e.g. 1200 dpi).

RFS (Radio Frequency System) A technology used to control lights where control signals are passed by radio rather than cable. It has the advantage of not requiring line-of-sight between the transceiver and device.

RGB (Red, Green, Blue) The primary colors of the additive model, used in monitors and image-editing programs.

rim-lighting Light from the side and behind a subject which falls on the edge (hence rim) of the subject.

ring-flash A lighting device with a hole in the center so that the lens can be placed through it, resulting in shadow-free images.

satellite In lighting, this is a parabolic dish designed to reflect and diffuse light.

saturation The purity of a color, going from the lightest tint to the deepest, most saturated tone.

scrim a light open-weave fabric, used to cover softboxes.

selection In image-editing, a part of an on-screen image that is chosen and defined by a border in preparation for manipulation or movement.

shutter The device inside a conventional camera that controls the length of time during which the film is exposed to light. Many digital cameras don't have a shutter, but the term is still used as shorthand to describe the electronic mechanism that controls the length of exposure for the CCD.

shutter speed The time the shutter (or electronic switch) leaves the CCD or film open to light during an exposure.

SLR (Single Lens Reflex) A camera that transmits the same image via a mirror to the film and viewfinder, ensuring that you get exactly what you see in terms of focus and composition.

slow sync The technique of firing the flash in conjunction with a slow shutter speed (as in rear-curtain sync).

snoot A tapered barrel attached to a lamp in order to concentrate the light emitted into a spotlight.

soft-box A studio lighting accessory consisting of a flexible box that attaches to a light source at one end and has an adjustable diffusion screen at the other, softening the light and any shadows cast by the subject.

spot meter A specialized light meter, or function of the camera light meter, that takes an exposure reading for a precise area of a scene.

sync cord The electronic cable used to connect camera and flash.

telephoto A photographic lens with a long focal length that enables distant objects to be enlarged. The drawbacks include a limited depth of field and angle of view.

TIFF (Tagged Image File Format) A file format for bitmapped images. It supports cmyk, rgb and grayscale files with alpha channels, and lab, indexed-color, and it can use LZW lossless compression. It is now the most widely used standard for good-resolution digital photographic images.

top lighting Lighting from above, useful in product photography since it removes reflections.

TTL (Through The Lens) Describes metering systems that use the light passing through the lens to evaluate exposure details.

tungsten A metalic element, used as the fillament for lightbulbs, hence tungsten lighting.

umbrella In photographic lighting umbrellas with reflective surfaces are used in conjunction with a light to diffuse the beam.

vapor discharge light A lighting technology common in stores and street lighting. It tends to produce color casts, especially the orange sodium vapor lights.

watt-seconds A measure of lighting power. One watt-second (Ws) is exactly equivalent to one Joule (a more common measure in Europe). Because this is a scientific measure of the energy used by the light, rather than light output, it can sometimes be misleading. For example, a focussed spot using the same energy as a diffused light would be much brighter as all the energy is concentrated into a small beam of light.

white balance A digital camera control used to balance exposure and color settings for artificial lighting types.

window light A softbox, typically rectangular (in the shape of a window) and suitably diffused.

zoom A camera lens with an adjustable focal length, giving, in effect, a range of lenses in one. Drawbacks include a smaller maximum aperture and increased distortion over a prime lens (one with a fixed focal length).

INDEX

INDEX

INDEX

BIBLIOGRAPHY AND USEFUL ADDRESSES

BOOKS

Digital imaging and photography

The Complete Guide to Digital Photography
Michael Freeman, *Lark*, New York 2002

Digital Photography Expert Series:

Close Up (2004)

Light and Lighting (2003)

Nature and Landscape (2004)

Portrait (2003)

All by Michael Freeman, *Lark*, New York

The Digital SLR Handbook
Michael Freeman, *Lark*, New York 2005

On the Road with your Digital Camera
Michael Freeman, *Thomson*, New York 2004

Creative Photoshop Lighting Techniques
Barry Huggins, *Lark*, New York 2004

Mastering Black and White Digital Photography
Michael Freeman, *Lark*, New York 2005

Mastering Color Digital Photography
Michael Freeman, *Lark*, New York 2005

WEB SITES

Note that Website addresses may often change, and sites appear and disappear with alarming regularity. Use a search engine to help find new arrivals or check addresses.

Photoshop sites (tutorials, information, galleries)

Absolute Cross Tutorials (including plug-ins) www.absolutecross.com/tutorials/photoshop.htm

Laurie McCanna's Photoshop Tips www.mccannas.com/pshop/photosh0.htm

Planet Photoshop (portal for all things Photoshop) www.planetphotoshop.com

Ultimate Photoshop www.ultimate-photoshop.com

Digital imaging and photography sites

Creativepro.com (e-magazine) www.creativepro.com

Digital Photography www.digital-photography.org

Digital Photography Review (digital cameras) www.dpreview.com

ShortCourses (digital photography: theory and practice) www.shortcourses.com

Software

Photoshop, Photoshop Elements, Photodeluxe www.adobe.com

Paintshop Pro, Photo-Paint, CorelDRAW! www.corel.com

PhotoImpact, PhotoExpress www.ulead.com

Toast Titanium www.roxio.com

USEFUL ADDRESSES

Adobe (Photoshop, Illustrator) www.adobe.com

Agfa www.agfa.com

Alien Skin (Photoshop Plug-ins) www.alienskin.com

Apple Computer www.apple.com

Association of Photographers (UK) www.aop.org

Corel (Photo-Paint, Draw, Linux) www.corel.com

Digital camera review www.dpreview.com

Epson www.epson.co.uk www.epson.com

Extensis www.extensis.com

Formac www.formac.com

Fractal www.fractal.com

Fujifilm www.fujifilm.com

Hasselblad www.hasselblad.se

Hewlett-Packard www.hp.com

Iomega www.iomega.com

Kodak www.kodak.com

Linotype www.linotype.org

LaCie www.lacie.com

Luminos (paper and processes) www.luminos.com

Macromedia (Director) www.macromedia.com

Microsoft www.microsoft.com

Nikon www.nikon.com

Nixvue www.nixvue.com

Olympus
www.olympusamerica.com
www.olympus.co.uk

Paintshop Pro www.jasc.com

Pantone www.pantone.com

Philips www.philips.com

Photographic information site www.ephotozine.com

Photoshop tutorial sites www.planetphotoshop.com
www.ultimate-photoshop.com

Polaroid www.polaroid.com

Qimage Pro www.ddisoftware.com/qimage/

Ricoh www.ricoh-europe.com

Samsung www.samsung.com

Sanyo www.sanyo.co.jp

Shutterfly (Digital Prints via the web) www.shutterfly.com

Sony www.sony.com

Sun Microsystems www.sun.com

Symantec www.symantec.com

Umax www.umax.com

Wacom (graphics tablets) www.wacom.com